DEVELOPING NEW FINANCIAL PRODUCTS

From Needs Analysis To Profitable Rollout

by
Gary H. Raddon
Raddon Financial Group

Financial Sourcebooks
Naperville, Illinois

Financial Sourcebooks
A Division of Sourcebooks, Inc.
P.O. Box 313
Naperville, Illinois, 60566

Cover design by Creative Mind Services.

This publication is designed to provide accurate and authoritative information in regard to the subject matter covered. It is sold with the understanding that the publisher is not engaged in rendering legal, accounting, or other professional service. If legal advice or other expert assistance is required, the services of a competent professional person should be sought.

From a Declaration of Principles Jointly Adopted by a Committee of the American Bar Association and a Committee of Publishers and Associations

Library of Congress Cataloging-in-Publication Data

Raddon, Gary H., 1935-
     Developing new financial products: from needs analysis to
  profitable rollout / by Gary H. Raddon.
          p.   cm.
     ISBN 0-942061-05-5   : $69.95
     1. Financial services industry.   2. New products.   I. Title.
  HG173.R34   1990
  332.1--dc20   89-28981
                                                                        CIP

Printed and bound in the United States of America

Table of Contents

Table of Contents

Table of Contents

Foreword

The financial services industry has undergone dramatic changes from regulatory, technological, cultural, and economic forces. One of the most dramatic results of these many changes is the need for financial service firms to be more marketing-oriented.

Marketing-oriented firms place an emphasis on their customers' needs and desires, and determine how customers' needs can be profitably served. A necessary ingredient of a marketing orientation is a strong program for developing new products. In the past, regulators controlled product and pricing decisions in the industry. The deregulated environment places the responsibility of product development on each individual firm. A discussion of these changes and their impact on the industry is found in Chapter 1.

This book provides an overview of the product development process for financial institutions. The book will take users through the necessary steps in product development, from strategic and product planning through product rollout and evaluation—Chapters 2-4.

Chapter 5, on profitability, is a guide that will help the user understand how to measure profit on an individual product level for explicit decision-making about product pricing. Market segment and relationship-pricing information provides a basis for understanding the industry's shift toward relationship pricing and marketing efforts, and their influence on product development.

The information on pricing strategy, Chapter 6, provides not only a philosophical background for new product-pricing decisions but also a framework for achieving marketing objectives with existing products. The chapter on product communication strategy, Chapter 7, and the case studies, Chapter 8, help the user understand how all the elements of product development can fit together in a product rollout.

1

Foreword

Included in this book are many checklists and planning formats that can be used directly in an organization's product development efforts. National consumer research data are included to help the reader gain an understanding of market segmentation, market needs, and how research can translate needs into product features and benefits—Appendices A-D.

Chapter 1

Banking—An Industry in Transition

Government Deregulation
Technological Change
Cultural and Demographic Change
Economic Climate Change
Industry Consolidation
New Competitive Challengers
Managing for Change
Summary

Chapter 1

Banking—An Industry in Transition

The financial industry is in the midst of a major transition period that is expected to last into the early 1990s. The financial industry of the 1990s will look very different from the way it looked during the 1980s.

The dynamics of this change are rooted in several fundamental transition forces: government deregulation, technological change, cultural and demographic change, change in the economic climate, industry consolidation, and new competitive challengers. Individually, each of these transition forces have influenced the financial industry. When they converge, these collective transition forces will dramatically change the industry's competitive face in the years ahead (See Exhibit 1.1).

Government Deregulation

Government deregulation is the catalyst for change in the financial industry. A more permissive regulatory structure has given birth to a new competitive environment—a competitive environment that assumes a more aggressive posture in response to the gray areas of regulatory interpretation.

Deregulation has forced many financial institutions to restructure their balance sheet and to reassess their competitive positioning. Management in many institutions continues to focus on a series of underlying balance sheet problems. These problems often include fixed-rate loan portfolios that are supported by market-rate-sensitive deposits, and/or extensive loan portfolios in numerous economically depressed industries and foreign countries.

Deregulation, together with technology, has redefined the scope of the traditional marketplace for financial institutions of all sizes, in particular the larger ones. Today, competition is just as likely to be viewed from a regional or national perspective as it is from a local one. The establish-

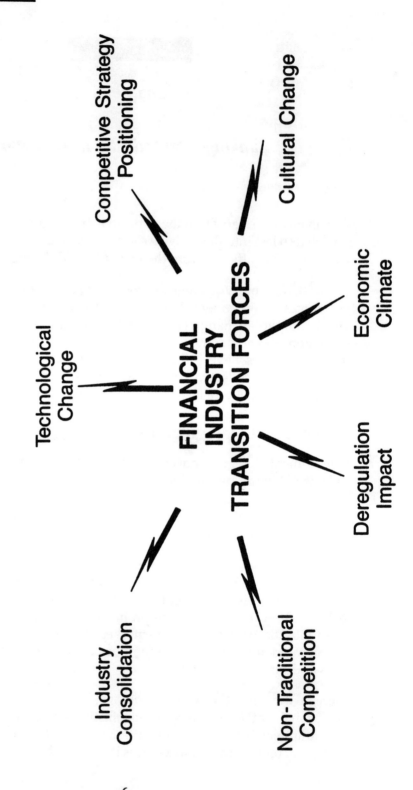

EXHIBIT 1.1
FINANCIAL INDUSTRY TRANSITION FORCES

Competitive Strategy Positioning

Cultural Change

Technological Change

FINANCIAL INDUSTRY TRANSITION FORCES

Economic Climate

Deregulation Impact

Industry Consolidation

Non-Traditional Competition

ment of competitive beachheads or new sales channels that operate outside an institution's traditional geographic boundaries has become commonplace within the financial industry.

Technological Change

Automation within the financial industry has come of age. It is moving out of the confines of a back-office operation onto the front lines of customer interface. Branch networks and sales distribution networks are being converted into "electronic railroads" that functionally integrate all aspects of the operation from the front-line, customer-contact point to the traditional back-office functions.

Regional and national distribution and sales channels have begun to emerge in a competitive role as well. Fully electronic sales and service delivery networks promise to provide a more-efficient and cost-effective sales production channel and customer service alternative in the future. Reducing the cost of personnel for both the acquisition and servicing of customers will ultimately be a requirement for remaining competitive in both price and service within the financial industry in the decade ahead.

Resistance to the electronic handling of financial transactions is fading. Consumers, particularly those younger and more affluent are rapidly becoming accustomed to electronic transactions as a way of handling their financial business. Perhaps equally important, financial institutions themselves are becoming more aware of the necessity to incorporate "high-tech" with "high-touch" if they are to maintain a competitive edge in the future. By the late 1990s, most routine financial transactions will probably be handled electronically.

Cultural and Demographic Change

Cultural and demographic change has become an increasingly pervasive force in all aspects of consumerism. Consumer activism is now less based on morality and is more centered on pragmatic economic issues. Today's consumer activism is expressed in a dedication to finding a better way to use the system and a willingness to circumvent or bypass traditional consumer sales channels.

Yesterday's "smart shoppers" were perceived as cost-savings conscious. Today's "smart shoppers" can more readily be described as cost-containment sensitive. They place greater value on leveraging their personal time and efforts, as long as major economic penalties are avoided. One-stop financial centers that focus on reducing consumer transaction time may become more appealing because of this new "smart-shopper" mentality. Still another characteristic is consumers' increasing utilization of national brand name products to ensure greater probability of making the right choice in their purchase decisions.

There also exists a trend back to older values. This trend is expressed in terms of more localistic, sometimes even parochial, thinking. It is further shown in the emergence of the importance of a sense of community, together with an even greater personal commitment and reliance on family, friends, and networking relationships.

The importance of these cultural changes is fueled by significant changes in the demographic mix of the country. Over 19 million new households are projected for the next decade. The financial industry is entering a decade of unprecedented demand for loans, with 20 million more people in the prime borrowing age group—thirty to fifty years of age. Diverse sub-segments of lifestyles exist within this same demographic age group; that is, divorced heads of households, young unmarrieds and dual-earner households. As a result, target market segmentation that is also product specific will become increasingly important in the decade ahead. The services of financial institutions will become more reflective of the different needs of their marketplace.

Economic Climate Change

The economic climate has changed dramatically during the last decade. Consumer savings rates and patterns have undergone an evolutionary, and at times a revolutionary, change. Consumers are saving less in the form of traditional deposits and expecting more in earnings' performance from their discretionary savings. Financial institutions are today paying the price for the high interest rates of the past. Financial institutions find themselves chasing fewer consumer savings dollars because consumers have grown increasingly aware of more-attractive investment alternatives, such as the stock market, mutual funds, and a variety of other tax-advantaged investment products. The premium savings interest rate yields offered by financial institutions still pale in comparison with the track record of the stock market and the interest rate yields to which consumers had become accustomed from their local financial institution in the early 1980s.

The financial industry is experiencing major trauma adjusting to a low-inflationary environment after operating for nearly a decade in a high-inflationary one. Many financial institutions' managers are not prepared to compete in an economic environment not driven by high inflation rates. Much of the financial industry's economic underpinning in terms of asset quality relied on the presumption of continued high inflation to offset any questionable lending practices. The obvious result is a record-setting number of financial institution failures and an even more-staggering number of financially crippled financial institutions.

The continued change in the tax codes and other tax-related issues has also eroded the financial strength of financial institutions of all types and sizes. Tax-code changes affecting the deductibility of interest and the eligibility requirements for IRAs may force a repositioning of many of the financial industry's products. After decades of operating under a tax-code umbrella that provided protection and positive support, financial institutions are being increasingly forced to rely upon their own management and competitive savvy. Additional economic dislocation will occur before the financial industry fully adapts to these changes in the economic-operating environment.

Industry Consolidation

Just as occurred in numerous other deregulated industries, such as the airline and trucking industries, competitive pressures are eroding the financial industry's profit margins. High-growth marketplaces already experience fierce competition for the same deposit and loan dollars. All marketplaces will experience vigorous competition for selective market segments that traditionally have yielded or, have promised to become, the most profitable customer relationships.

Competitive pressures force consolidation in the financial industry as institutions seek to create sustainable economies of scale or competitive advantages in their distribution network. The size and geographic scope of a financial institution's distribution system is more important than ever. Risk-management strategies are increasingly predicated upon an institution's financial muscle to withstand the vagaries of interest rate movements. More sophisticated electronic information systems facilitate the expansion of the major regional and national financial institutions. As pricing competition increases for profitable depository and lending relationships, the competitive advantage oftentimes swings toward those financial institutions with a greater geographic market reach and a more cost-effective distribution system.

The middle-size financial institutions continue to be absorbed through a wave of intrastate and interstate mergers and acquisitions. Survivors are beginning to cluster at either the customer-servicing or asset-leveraging ends of the financial industry spectrum. Local and specialist financial institutions are expected to survive by carving out niches where they can create and sustain a competitive advantage for themselves.

New Competitive Challengers

Deregulation and technological change are creating new sales and service distribution channels for financial services. A new group of competitive challengers has emerged for the old guard of financial industry players as a result of the opportunities presented by these shifts in sales and service distribution channels.

The new challengers are from nonfinancial industry companies, national financial-industry-related networks, and companies in the franchising industry that have diversified. Nonfinancial industry companies view their diversification into the financial industry as an opportunity to either leverage an in-place regional/national distribution system or their expertise in operating distribution systems with great geographic scope. Since "lowest cost" is often their sustaining competitive advantage, the development of multirevenue streams for their sunk-cost distribution networks can be utilized to offset the high cost associated with the maintenance of them. Sears, General Motors, K-Mart, Prudential, and the Ford Motor Company are examples of the new nontraditional competitors who will help reshape the financial industry during the 1990s.

Another noteworthy group of potentially influential competitors are national real estate broker networks. Century 21, ERA, Realty World, Coldwell Banker, and Merrill Lynch will be among the leaders of this group. These new competitors pursue strategies of vertical integration, pivoting around their control of the home-buying transaction point. Real estate companies are attempting to leverage this control into additional fee-income opportunities by offering mortgage lending, insurance services, and real estate transaction-related investment alternatives. The tremendous potential for generation of revenue afforded through a successful vertical-integration strategy provides the necessary incentive to overcome any initial problems and setbacks encountered during efforts to gain entry to these additional lines of business.

The concept of franchising services could gather momentum and further change the competitive complexion of the industry at some point in the future. Franchising is the great equalizer in most industries, particularly those that are service based. The business format concept of franchising allows businesses to get into limited banking-related service (i.e. consumer mortgage lending) with minimal or no prior experience. The initial wave of franchisees will be real estate brokers and small mortgage brokerage firms. Eventually, financial institutions will affiliate with franchise networks or co-op groups as well. While franchise banking concepts such as First Interstate Bank and the "banker's bank" co-ops have met limited or no financial success, financial institutions should not overlook their potential to create financial and competitive advantages. These prospective advantages continue to drive the search for the right financial and competitive ingredients to make such concepts viable.

Finally, some competitors will go directly to the consumer, by utilizing a national brand name recognition strategy to bypass more costly distribution systems. Numerous firms are engaged in such efforts including Citicorp, Prudential-Bache, Sears, and American Express. The concept of marketing specific financial services directly to consumers is in its embryonic stage of development. Although these efforts have not yet produced any spectacular financial success stories, this trend merits continued observation because it represents the ultimate low-cost competitive strategy.

Managing for Change

The changes that these transition forces have brought to the financial industry present a clearcut challenge to the executive management of every financial institution. The challenge is simply this:

Your financial institution must do business "differently"
in the
- "Minds" of management
- "Actions" of service personnel
- "Hearts" of the sales force
- "Eyes" of the consumer

The product development process, one of the key, and most visible, elements to be utilized by management in meeting this challenge, is the subject of the remainder of this book.

Banking—An Industry in Transition

Summary

The financial industry is undergoing a transformation as a result of government deregulation, technological change, cultural and demographic change, economic climate change, industry consolidation, and the emergence of new competitive challengers. These transition forces are changing the nature of permissible financial services, service delivery alternatives, customer expectations and decision-making rationale, capital and financial performance requirements, the geographic scope of competition, and sales channel perspectives for financial services.

The resultant changes in the characteristics of the financial industry hold significant implications for the product development function and its role in bridging the gaps in the way institutions manage these changes. The product development process deals with the issues that drive the changes in the financial industry.

The product development process has been informally practiced, if practiced at all, in most financial institutions. Management decisions about product line must be resolved within the framework of financial conditions, market opportunities, and the customer base of each financial institution. The financial industry's transition forces present an endless array of choices for executive management. How management elects to respond to the choices presented may well determine the long-term survival prospects of individual financial institutions. The product development process provides the structure for management to execute a workable transitional strategy.

Chapter 2

Product Development—
A Dynamic Management Process

Chapter 2

Product Development—
A Dynamic Management Process

The Strategic Plan Link

Product development is a dynamic extension of management's execution of the strategic business plan's goals and objectives. The product development process provides a structured path for the creation and management of a financial service product line. The product line supports the accomplishment of earnings, market share, and quality service-performance objectives at an acceptable level of risk to the financial institution. Exhibit 2.1—The Strategic Plan Link— illustrates this linkage between the financial institution's product-line strategy and its strategic business plan.

The institution's products tactical plans, which form the basis for product-line planning and management, are actually an outgrowth of a series of business-planning stages. The product's tactical plans help drive the institution's actions to achieve its strategic business statement objectives.

Product Planning and Management Loop

Product-line planning and management encompasses two distinctly different functions—product development and existing product maintenance. It is the interaction between these two functions that makes product development a dynamic management process. Every product developed by the institution is transferred into the existing product maintenance function at some point during its life cycle. While the focus here is on product development, many of the issues addressed are interchangeable between both functions. Exhibit 2.2—The Product Planning and Management Loop—illustrates this interrelationship.

EXHIBIT 2.1
THE STRATEGIC PLAN LINK

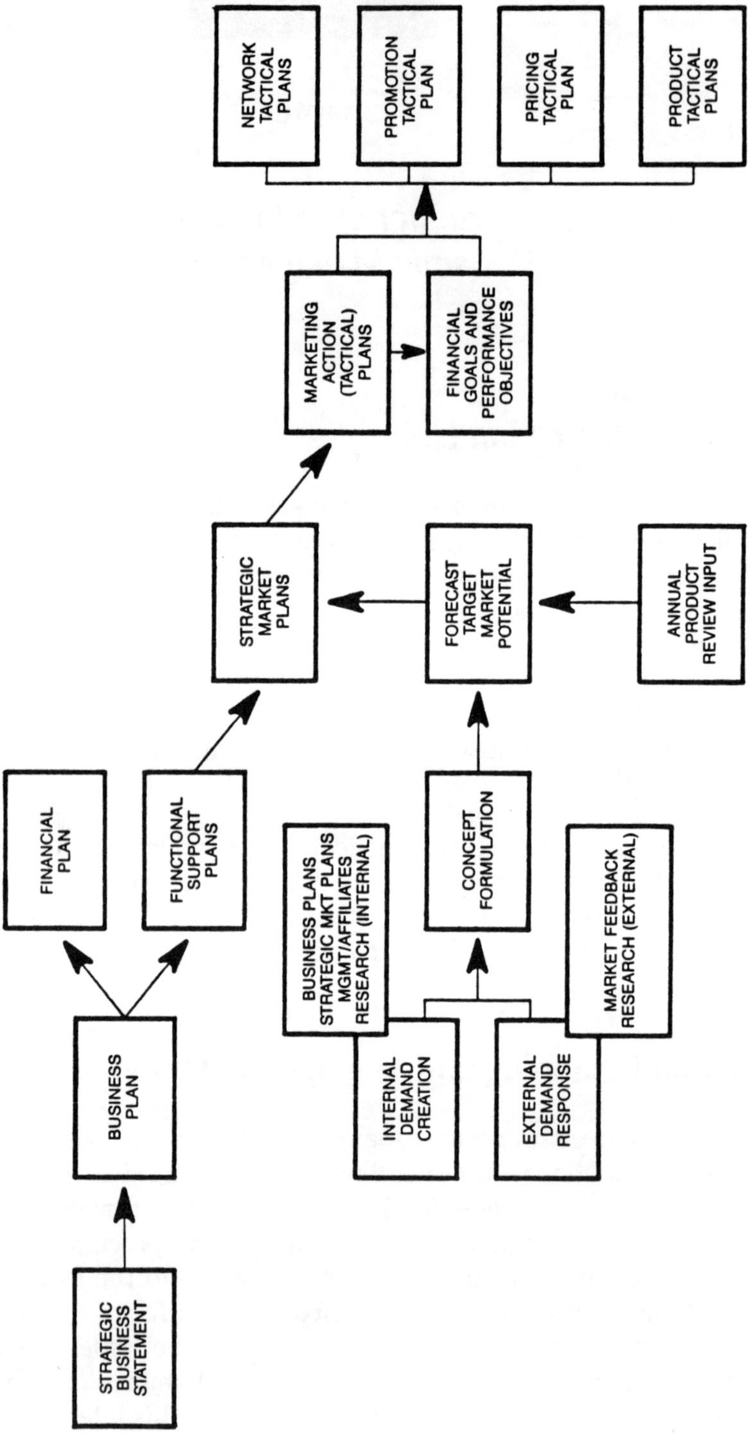

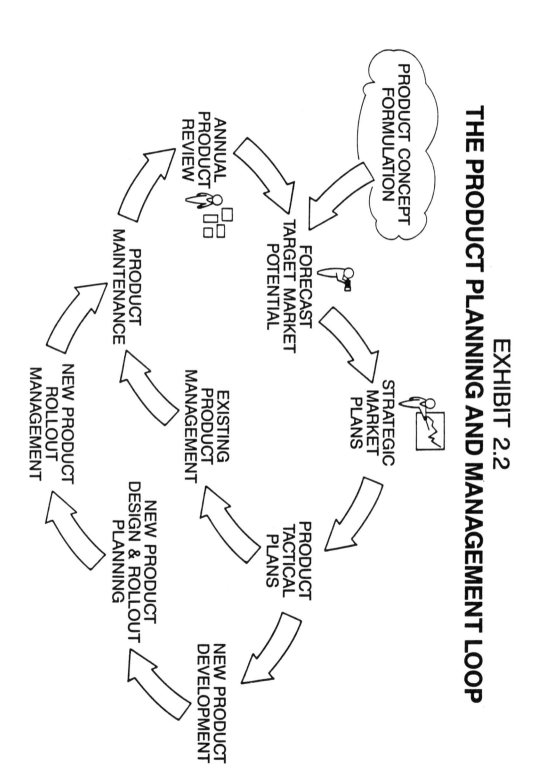

EXHIBIT 2.2

THE PRODUCT PLANNING AND MANAGEMENT LOOP

PRODUCT CONCEPT FORMULATION

FORECAST TARGET MARKET POTENTIAL

ANNUAL PRODUCT REVIEW

PRODUCT MAINTENANCE

NEW PRODUCT ROLLOUT MANAGEMENT

NEW PRODUCT DESIGN & ROLLOUT PLANNING

EXISTING PRODUCT MANAGEMENT

NEW PRODUCT DEVELOPMENT

PRODUCT TACTICAL PLANS

STRATEGIC MARKET PLANS

The Product Development Function

The product development process within financial institutions should vary only in terms of the resources devoted to it, not in its functional structure. For example, larger financial institutions often have specialized staffs and more sophisticated database resource to devote to the process than do smaller institutions. However, the function of the process does not vary among financial institutions.

In smaller financial institutions, the product development function is coordinated within the management area of general marketing, or in the absence of dedicated marketing personnel, it may be coordinated within the institution's marketing committee group. In larger institutions, the function will have one or more full-time management and staff personnel dedicated to it.

In virtually all instances, the product development function has a coordinating rather than a technical role. Exhibit 2.3—Overview of the Product Development Function—indicates that the product development function crosses numerous management support disciplines within the institution: operations, finance, human resources, legal, and marketing. It's role is to focus and coordinate the institution's resources during the rollout of financial products/services.

Product Development Rollout

The product development function's multidiscipline coordination role is summarized in Exhibit 2.4—Product Development Rollout. This coordination role can be performed by a task force group, committee, or product manager, depending upon an organization's resources and/or management culture. It is only critical that accountability for the coordination role exist somewhere within the organization.

The product development process originates at the development stage of the strategic market plan. It is at this stage in the strategic business-planning process that "demand" for product development initially surfaces.

The demand for products can be internally created by business plan objectives, strategic market plans, management, or internal research. Similarly, demand for a product is generated in response to marketplace feedback and/or research activities. These sources of demand for product development feed into the development of strategic market plans and, subsequently, tactical marketing plans.

EXHIBIT 2.3
OVERVIEW OF THE PRODUCT DEVELOPMENT FUNCTION

MARKETING	FINANCE	OPERATIONS	LEGAL	HUMAN RESOURCES
1. IDENTIFY CUSTOMERS				
2. RESEARCH DESIRED PRODUCT BENEFITS				
3. DESIGN PRODUCT		3. PARTICIPATE IN PRODUCT DESIGN	3. PARTICIPATE IN PRODUCT DESIGN	
4. PRICE PRODUCT FOR MAXIMUM PROFIT	4. PARTICIPATE IN PRICING		4. PARTICIPATE IN PRICING	
5. TEST PRODUCT FOR PROFIT AND PERFORMANCE	5. PARTICIPATE IN TESTING AND MONITOR PROFIT	5. PARTICIPATE IN TESTING		5. IDENTIFY TRAINING SUPPORT REQUIREMENTS
6. RECEIVE MANAGEMENT APPROVAL AND ROLLOUT PRODUCT PER TEST	6. PRODUCE THE PRODUCT TO MEET DESIGN STANDARDS	6. PRODUCE THE PRODUCT TO MEET DESIGN STANDARDS		6. PRODUCE TRAINING MATERIALS & PROVIDE TRAINING SUPPORT
7. PROMOTE AND DISTRIBUTE PRODUCT				
8. SOLICIT ORDERS FROM CUSTOMERS FOR PRODUCT	8. MONITOR PROFIT			
9. MONITOR CHANGES IN DESIRED BENEFITS				
10. TRACK COMPETITION				

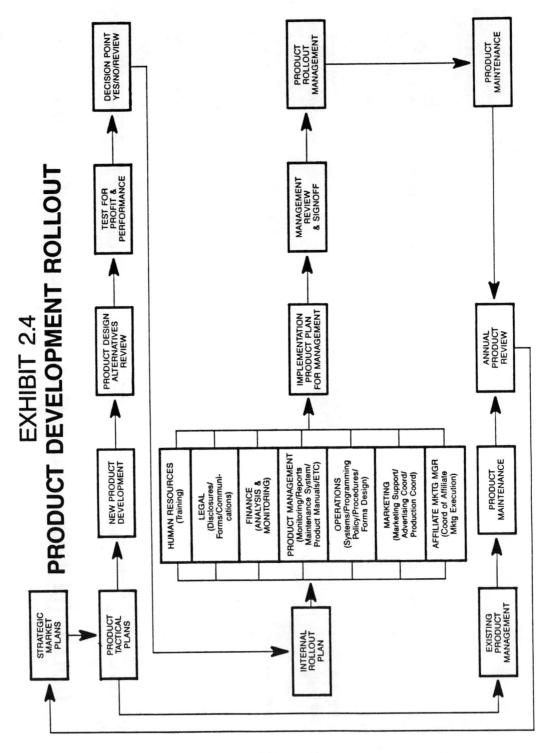

EXHIBIT 2.4
PRODUCT DEVELOPMENT ROLLOUT

The actual product development process itself is given birth within the traditional "4Ps" of marketing—product, price, promotion, and place (distribution). Concepts and forecasts of target market potential for a product are generally developed at this stage of the planning process.

Management's decision to proceed with further development of a concept for a product is implicitly given by its inclusion within the product's tactical plans, created to support the institution's strategic marketing plans. Product development is more formalized once it reaches the written stage of product tactical plans. Product concept acceptance and market potential forecasts are examined during the process of developing alternative product design for management's review. These alternative designs are then tested for profit and performance prior to presentation to management for review and decision-making.

Once a product's design is approved by management, an internal rollout plan is created. It is at this point that the product development process assumes a multidisciplined dimension, as shown in Exhibits 2.3 and 2.4. Operations gets involved in designing systems, programming modifications, developing policies and procedures, and creating forms. Finance assists in the financial analysis and in the establishment of any required monitoring mechanism. Human resources determines training materials and provides training support. Legal advises in the legal and regulatory review, as well as in the development of required disclosures, forms, and communications. Marketing provides the research, communication, promotion, pricing, production, and delivery supports. Distribution network management coordinates implementation within branches, affiliates, or subsidiaries if applicable.

The product development function pulls all of these activities together into a product's implementation plan for management's review and sign-off. After a product's implementation has been approved by management, the product development function manages the product's rollout. Products are then handed off to the appropriate groups for ongoing maintenance support. An annual product review should be conducted of the product line, with specific product review feedback and recommendations looped back into the business-planning process during the development of strategic market plans.

Product development requires the identification of financial service needs within the marketplace and the quantification of market potential that is associated with the satisfaction of those needs. Financial institutions must understand when and how to use market research, both primary and secondary, to develop the required information and data. This is of equal or even greater importance than having whoever is responsible for managing the product development function understand how to apply the information from a strategic perspective in product development.

There are four strategic elements in product development: the product design, the offer, the promotion media, and the delivery channel. Each is integral to a successful product rollout, however great or small the scope. Financial institutions must constantly fight the tendency to emphasize one of these elements at the expense of another.

Product design can encompass building a new product from "scratch" or repositioning an existing product. It can also simply involve enhancement of a product's perceived value through packaging or a premium offer.

The *offer element* encompasses selecting the pricing mechanism and using the marketplace's "price-band" parameters to manipulate customer demand. In setting the price, the offer should reflect price break points whenever appropriate.

The *promotion media element* should be driven by the product's targeted market segments. Media selection criteria should reflect the most cost-effective per-sale index, as determined by pilot testing whenever possible. The creative strategy employed in promoting the product is one of the most flexible elements in the development of the product strategy formulation process.

Delivery channel selection is the final element of the product strategy formulation process. It requires the identification of the most cost-efficient channels—direct and/or indirect—to reach the product's targeted market segments.

The Product's Marketing Plan

It is not uncommon for entrepreneur executives to introduce new products without a written marketing plan. The absence of a written plan limits the receipt from others of potentially valuable insights that might make a product more successful, or at least less likely to fail. The

Exhibit 2.5

The Product Marketing Plan's Format

Plan Name:	**Time Period:** **Preparer:** **Date:**
Introduction:	Who, how and why plan prepared; scope of data
Product Description:	Features, benefits, positioning and possible variations
Marketing Environment:	Competitive positioning, pricing, promotional, distribution, operational, legal, and other known issues
Market Potential:	Demographic/psychographic data, prospective market-place demand, market extension options
Strategies:	Goals, objectives, strategic alternatives, and recommendations with rationale
Implementation:	Key tasks/activities, time frames, resource commitments, projected results, and performance measurement criteria
Optional Addendum:	a. Question and answer supplement b. Forms/procedures/policies supplement

basic elements of any product marketing plan are the product description, marketing environment, objective statement, and strategies to be employed. Exhibit 2.5—The Product Marketing Plan's Format—outlines a basic plan's components.

It is important for management to track the progress in implementation throughout the product development rollout process. Exhibit 2.6—

EXHIBIT 2.6

Action Plan Overview

Date: _____ **, 199__**

ACTION PLAN NAME: _____ I D# _____

SUBJECT REFERENCE: _____

_____

_____ I D# _____

STRATEGICAL APPROACH: _____

_____

_____

RESOURCE REQUIREMENTS: _____

_____

KEY PROGRESS CHECKPOINTS:

CHECKPOINT DESCRIPTION	ASSIGNED	PLAN SCHEDULE DATES			
		Start-Up	Progress Check	Projected Completion	Actual Completion

EXHIBIT 2.6a

Detailed Action Plan Schedule Summary

Week of:_____; Date: _____, 199__

PROJECT/TASK DESCRIPTION								

Product Development

Action Plan Overview—and Exhibit 2.6a—Detailed Action Plan Schedule Summary—provide a snapshot documentation of the anticipated rollout project schedule. These support documents for the marketing plan should be prepared for each product development project so that management can monitor the completion of key progress, checkpoint-related tasks or activities.

Summary

Product development is a dynamic extension of the institution's strategic business plan that helps the institution achieve stated goals and objectives. The product planning and management loop does not functionally vary, regardless of an institution's size.

The role of the product development function is to both focus and coordinate the institution's resources during the rollout of financial services products. In that role, the product development function involves numerous management support disciplines, including operations, finance, human resources, legal, and marketing.

Demand for product development surfaces during the development stages of the strategic marketing plan. Internal demand for product development is created by business plan objectives, strategic market plans, management results, or internal research. External demand for product development is generated in response to the marketplace, and/or primary research findings.

The four strategic elements of product development are product design, the offer element, the promotion media element, and delivery channel selection. All are equally important to the successful rollout of any product that is developed.

The basic elements of the product's written marketing plan are the product description, marketing environment assessment, an objective statement, and a synopsis of the strategies to be employed. This self-contained document provides management with the relevant background information for evaluating the merit of the product development concept and for making a judgment about committing resources to it.

The product's rollout plan has a multidisciplined dimension that encompasses operations, finance, human resources, legal, marketing, and distribution network management. Tracking the progress of the plan's implementation requires the preparation and maintenance of an overview that details key progress checkpoints, and the tasks or activities related to each. This helps assure management of the timely completion of product development projects within the plan's allotted financial, timing, and personnel resources constraints.

Chapter 3

Market Research Role—
Identifying Needs and Quantifying Opportunity

Employee Opinion—An Overlooked Resource for
New Product Ideas
Product Evaluation Matrix
Qualitative Research—Consumer Focus Groups
Quantitative Research
Evaluating Opportunities for New Products
Market Segmentation—
The Product Development Process
Consumer Needs Analysis
Summary

Chapter 3

Market Research Role—
Identifying Needs and Quantifying Opportunity

As already observed in this book, many elements are required to create an environment for successful product development. Continued success of new products can be correlated to having the commitment and support of top management in identifying, monitoring, and analyzing the changing financial needs of the consumer in today's marketplace.

This commitment requires a research-driven organization. Not infrequently, organizations look upon product research as a one-time effort rather than as an ongoing process. Successful product development requires funding a generous research budget year in and year out, even when there is downturn in profit margins. Research and development (R & D) budgets for new products are normally the first ones to be cut when management focus is on controlling expense rather than on generating revenue.

New product ideas can come from many sources, depending on the research technique. Marketing, operations, management, customers, noncustomers, employees, competitors, and advertising agencies alike are all important resources for ideas on new products. However, most ideas for new products come from the marketplace and are closely related to an institution's primary line of business. In recent years, the marketplace has observed the expansion of savings and investment product lines with the introduction of high-rate passbook savings accounts, stock market (S&P 500) certificates, annuities, and mutual funds. Credit products have been expanded to include variable-rate consumer loans, home-equity lines and loans, biweekly installment loans, biweekly mortgages, and mortgages that promise quick closing dates.

Transaction products are constantly changing with the packaging of various types of checking plans, from senior citizen programs to high-income, preferred-customer programs. Occasionally, the firm begins, or acquires, an entirely new product line such as a travel agency business, mortgage banking, or a real estate brokerage business.

The success of these products and/or businesses depends on a complete and comprehensive approach to market research. Too frequently management will rely on "gut feelings" and third-party testimonies as the primary research technique for gathering data. Although such considerations are important, these short-cut approaches can become rather expensive, particularly if the product isn't successful. Product research and development doesn't eliminate the risk, but it can quantify the product's opportunity in terms of market acceptance and profitability.

Employee Opinion— An Overlooked Resource for New Product Ideas

Establishing an open forum for the exchange of ideas between management and front line employees is a key element in the research process. Management's interests in "new ideas" can be communicated throughout the organization by employee focus groups. Using employee focus groups improves the working climate for employees and provides better customer service.

Sometimes employee research will focus on a specific issue such as high-rate savings passbooks, or biweekly mortgages. While at other times, management may not have a specific product in mind but is more concerned with dealing with broader issues such as asset and liability management or increasing fee-income.

Discussing and resolving these broader issues is somewhat more challenging than focusing on a specific product. However, the results of this kind of effort can be very beneficial if the climate for discussion is positive and if employees are encouraged to participate regardless of how "off-the-wall" the suggestion might be.

The following questions can be helpful in encouraging employee participation in focus group discussions aimed at generating new ideas for product development:

- If you could make one change here at the institution that would either make your job easier to do or would provide better service to the customer, what would it be?

- Many new products and services are being introduced in the marketplace. These new products, as well as existing banking services, are often confusing to the customer. Based on your contact with customers and your personal experience, what one topic should be discussed to clear up any confusion about products?

- What, do you feel, is the institution's greatest competitive weakness?

- What do you feel is the institution's greatest competitive strength? Please limit your response to one service that you feel is the single-most-important one for the institution's success.

- Please list the customer-service activities that you perform during a typical working day that in your opinion, take more time than necessary to complete to the customer's satisfaction. Please explain why the transaction takes so much time.

- What new service or product do you feel the institution should provide for customers in the coming year, and why?

Product Evaluation Matrix

Management, as well as frontline employees, can assist the institution in evaluating its existing product structure. A useful exercise is to use the General Electric Model for evaluating various products (see Exhibit 3.1 on the following page). Along the horizontal axis, the employee rates the attractiveness of the product in the marketplace as either high, medium, or low. Along the vertical axis, the employee rates the product in terms of the firm's competitive strength in marketing the product. In *Marketing Financial Services*, by Donnelly, Berry, and Thompson, some of the components of *competitive strength* included: institution size, share of market, customer loyalty, technology, personnel, image, reputation, cost structure, number and quality of facilities, financial strength, and management capability and capacity. The components of *market attractiveness* included: market size, market growth, types of competition, market stability, regulatory uncertainty, industry capacity, ratios of fixed costs to value added, cross-selling potential, substitution effects, bargaining power of customers, and ease of switching institutions.

Exhibit 3.1 contains an example of a product evaluation matrix in which employees evaluate their firm's product line. Such evaluations should be individual efforts which then can be summarized as the products are classified as either A, B, or C. Class A products are those which receive the highest priority in the institution in terms of marketing resources. These are the market development products. Class B products are the maintenance products. Market share and profitability should be sustained with the necessary ongoing marketing support. Class C products are of a lower priority. The firm should consider discontinuing the products in this category, unless changes in the products' structure, price, or delivery will enhance market opportunity and thus change the products classification to either A or B.

Exhibit 3.1

Market Attractiveness

		High	Medium	Low
C o m p e t i t i v e	**High**	NOW Regular checking Premium passbook **A**	Annuity One-year CD Unsecured personal line of credit **A**	 **B**

S t r e n g t h	**Medium**	MMDA
		CDs—6-month
		Self-directed IRA
		
		A
			Charge card
			Home equity
			Consumer credit
			  —auto
			Mortgage loans
			ATMs
			IRA
			Marine financing
			Mobile homes
			OD checking
			RVs
			B
				Full-line insurance
				  Health
				  Accident
				  Life
				
				C

	Low	Regular savings **B**	Senior citizen club **C**	Discount brokerage Safe-deposit box **C**

As observed in this particular example, the firm should evaluate these Class C products further: safe-deposit boxes, discount brokerage, insurance, and the senior citizen club. This approach immediately prioritizes existing R&D efforts.

However, employee perceptions of opportunities for product may or may not accurately reflect consumer perceptions. Thus, the next step in the process is to take what has been learned from employees and match it with consumer reactions. There are several ways to accomplish this: consumer focus groups, direct-mail consumer panels, telephone surveys, and person-to-person interviews. Each research technique has its own unique characteristics when it comes to the product development process.

Qualitative Research—Consumer Focus Groups

One frequently used qualitative research technique for determining consumers reactions to products is the focus group. Focus groups bring together a group of consumers to discuss a concept or service in an open forum that allows for interaction and the exchange of ideas. How can financial institutions effectively use focus groups for research in their product development effort? The following are specific objectives for which focus groups can be used.

- *Assessing predisposition.* A focus group can be used to determine the predisposition of a group of consumers toward a particular concept. Consumer preferences for a new financial product, particular service, a method of delivery, or how previous advertising or promotional experiences influence decision-making can also be tested.

- *Testing preference.* The focus group can be offered a series of ideas and asked to indicate preferences for one of more of these choices. They can rank them in order of choice, choose one from among a set, or express their preferences for a particular product or financial institution in a variety of ways.

  These processes of determining preferences help estimate how a broader audience will react to such issues as a change in business practices, a change in packaging, a modification of features, or the expansion of a product line.

- *Discovering a process.* How does an individual make a decision or implement a process? How does an expert perform? What subject matter does the expert know? In many cases, this information can be obtained through a focus group.

- *Validating a process.* The focus group can be used to test an idea, to see if others are able to accept the idea and implement it properly.

A focus group is best used when a single objective for the group has been clearly defined. Any of the above objectives, or a range of others, might be suitable as a focus group's research objective. It is important, however, that *only one* objective be set for the focus group. For example, don't combine testing reaction to a new logo with testing reactions to a new product. Choose one narrowly defined objective.

Qualitative research can be extremely useful in defining the product concept. If market risk is minimal and consumer response in the focus group is very positive, the institution may move directly to implementing the product without the need for further research. However, normally the focus group will provide R&D with a number of research issues that will be quantified in further discussions with consumers.

Quantitative Research

There are three basic quantitative research approaches that can be used in enhancing the product development process: direct-mail consumer panels, telephone surveys, and personal interviews.

Direct-Mail Consumer Panels

Direct-mail panels are successfully used by firms that wish to gather, in a fast and efficient way, a great deal of financial information about the product idea. Complex concepts about the product can be tested with direct-mail panel respondents because they can be sent visual materials and detailed, written explanations to aid them in their consideration of a product.

Care should be taken in balancing the sampling process to include a slight overrepresentation of younger consumers. Older direct-mail panel members show a slightly higher tendency to complete financial questionnaires.

Sending direct-mail surveys to a firm's own customer base can be a cost-effective way to measure customer reaction to a new product or service. Institutions typically can expect a 20 percent rate of response on surveys mailed to customers where the financial institution is identified as the sponsor. A sample questionnaire is included in Appendix C. Direct mail to noncustomers also can be used to evaluate new products; however, the low rate of response can introduce an unacceptable level of nonresponse error.

When doing pricing research on a new product, it's more efficient to use direct-mail because it provides consumers with a variety of alternatives or options. From the responses, institutions can determine what pricing structure will work best in terms of profitability, market value, or product utility.

Telephone Surveys

Telephone interviewing is probably the most common research technique for new product development or for evaluating existing products. Normally, the caller can complete one-out-of-every-four calls; thus, the survey must have a fairly large telephone sample. This type of product research is fast and usually moderately priced.

However, there is more concern today about the quality of the call because of the great increase in telephone marketing over the past few years. The type of person who stays on the phone to answer a twelve minute questionnaire may not be representative of the marketplace.

Quality control is extremely important in this type of research. Callers must be periodically monitored. The sample of households should be randomly drawn, and callers should make four attempts to reach each member of the sample.

Personal Interviews

The personal interview is an excellent research technique. The more technical the product is, the more useful is this research technique. Normally, wholesale or commercial products, such as a new cash-management vehicle, require an in-depth, personal interview. The researcher interviews the prospective end user, who in the case of a new cash-management vehicle would be a relatively sophisticated user of cash-management services. This can be an expensive process because a representative number of consumers in the market must be recruited, compensated, and interviewed.

In-person, lobby-intercept interviews can provide management with a quick measure of customer opinions on a variety of topics. The length of the questionnaire generally must be kept under five minutes.

Data gathered in lobby-interecept studies are not generally projectable to a financial institution's customer base because the sample is over-representative of transaction-oriented customers. Loan and certificate customers have less chance of being included in a lobby-based study.

Competitive Research

Certainly one of the most cost-effective ways an organization can gain information is to regularly monitor and evaluate their competitors. Data that are reported to regulatory agencies are available in a variety of formats and provide insights on competitive performance and strategy. Systematic monitoring of competitive rates and fees gives an essential understanding of their overall pricing strategies.

Summary—Product Development Research

Regardless of the research technique, the objective of product development research is to accurately identify which product features the consumer perceives to have the greatest utility and to determine the value of that utility. Once these features have been identified, the marketer then develops a structure for the product to best fit the consumer's perceived needs.

Evaluating Opportunities for New Products

When assessing the size of the market opportunity, consumers can be asked how likely they would be to use the product. When using a rating scale with extremely likely, very likely, somewhat likely and not at all likely it's possible to forecast product demand. In Exhibit 3.2, consumers were asked about a biweekly mortgage.

A rule-of-thumb method for measuring market demand requires totaling the percent who are *extremely likely* (38%) and one-half of the percent of the *very likely* (8%). Thus, market demand for biweekly mortgage payment is estimated at 46% of those households planning on taking out a mortgage over the next twelve months. While this percentage could change as consumers obtain more information about the product, the research data in Exhibit 3.2 suggests that there is significant demand.

Exhibit 3.2

Biweekly Mortgage Loan Payment

Some lenders are offering a new type of mortgage that provides substantial interest savings. Instead of making monthly payments in the traditional way, you make payments of one-half your regular mortgage payment every other week. At the end of the year you'll have made the equivalent of thirteen traditional mortgage payments. With this biweekly mortgage, you will pay off your loan in just 20 years and decrease your interest expense by 25%. On a $50,000 mortgage, a biweekly mortgage could save over $40,000 in interest expense. How likely would you be to select a biweekly mortgage loan?

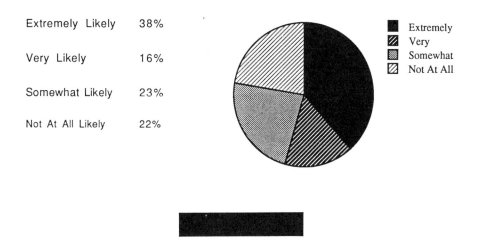

Extremely Likely	38%
Very Likely	16%
Somewhat Likely	23%
Not At All Likely	22%

Legend: Extremely, Very, Somewhat, Not At All

Using the existing market share of mortgage originations, the institution can project anticipated demand. With information on average mortgage balances and on the cost of mortgage origination, the institution can bring this market demand down to bottom-line performance. When research is used to quantify bottom-line performance for new opportunities for products, it then contributes significantly to a firm's profitability and minimizes the risks associated with marketing unprofitable products.

In addition to market demand and profitability, other key research issues must be resolved before determining the relative investment opportunities that a new product will bring to an institution. Some of the issues to be resolved in the research process are:

- *Differentiation potential.* Will the new product provide the institution with a strong market position? This position can be gauged by how attractive the marketplace finds the product and how unique the product is in the current marketplace.

- *Present competitive climate.* These data are available in the local market from secondary research. Shopping surveys of local competitors will identify what products are currently being marketed.

- *Future competitive trends.* Financial ratios can be used to predict competitors' reactions to marketplace developments. An understanding of financial strengths and weaknesses can tie into marketing strategy. Sometimes a competitor cannot react because of financial constraints. Competitive data on the cost of funds, earning-asset yield, and loan-to-deposit ratio are affordable for most institutions.

- *People resources.* Knowing the number of people required to support the product's development and ongoing implementation is a key issue, but more important is the skill required by this support team. Too often, good products fail because of a lack of support in maintaining the marketing and operations requirements of the product.

- *System/technology.* Almost any new product requires systems support. Many goods ideas die after considerable time has been spent on product development because software support was not available. Although this is an important research issue in product development, it should not become the driving force of product development. If this happens a firm will not have much of an incentive for developing new products. Begin with the market need, and then approach systems with the requirements of the product.

- *Capacity constraints.* In addition to people skills, the organization should have either excess capacity or a method for developing additional capacity to support the product. This consideration is particularly true for high-volume, transaction-type accounts. A product that might look good if a firm has excess capacity, could turn into a loser because of the costs associated with building additional capacity.

- *Regulatory climate.* For many products, the regulatory climate is becoming an important research issue. Monitoring new product development as a result of regulatory change, it is apparent that the industry is very much a product development follower. Therefore, it is important for financial institutions to get out in front of the regulations and try to predict what may happen in the future, so they can be on the leading edge of the change. In most new product opportunities, the leader in the marketplace is able to skim off some of the best, early adopter customers.

  Another area to research constantly is the re-regulation of pricing structures. Credit-card rates, home-equity application fees, NSF fees and payment of interests on investable funds all come under fire from consumer groups, which do have an impact on the legislative re-regulation process—particularly in the House of Representatives. Legislative, regulatory, and consumer group activity should be constantly monitored because of the impact that regulation has on profitability.

Many of these research issues are internal and can be analyzed using secondary data. Other issues require primary research. However, research, whether secondary or primary, is critical to the product development process. The greater the institution's research skills, the fewer mistakes it will make when bringing a product to the marketplace. Also, after the product has been launched, periodic assessment of the product's acceptance in the marketplace is required to fine-tune the process.

Market Segmentation— The Product Development Process

The objectives of market segmentation include, but not are limited to, the following:

- Channeling money and effort into the most profitable markets

- Structuring products that match market demands and are profitable for the institution

- Developing strategies that will enable an institution to selectively target markets with its products

- Improving the profitability of customer households

There are a wide variety of market segmentation approaches in the financial services industry. These include demographics, geo-demographics, lifestyle clustering, product usage, and life cycle. We will discuss some of these approaches briefly below.

Demographic Segmentation

Demographics refer to age, income, occupation, marital status, and other personal characteristics. Consumers' use of financial products is highly related to demographic characteristics. Age and income are the two customer characteristics most correlated with financial service usage. For example, national consumer research done in early 1987 for the FIMA/Raddon Strategic Research and Planning Program revealed that use of certificates of deposit increases dramatically with age. Persons sixty-five years old, or older are four times more likely to use a certificate of deposit than persons between eighteen and thirty-four. Thus, when developing a new certificate product or targeting new customer households for this type of product, the senior citizen market is a more-productive segment.

The Individual Retirement Account (IRA) is another good example of demographic correlation to financial product usage. Sixty-six percent of households earning $50,000 or more have an IRA while only 17 percent of households earning less than $25,000 use IRAs. Thus, high income households are four times more likely than lower income households to use IRAs.

Similar demographic correlations can be seen in consumers' usage of credit. Credit product usage generally declines after age forty-five and increases significantly with household income. The chapter on profitability analysis (Chapter 5) will show the dramatic differences in profit opportunities when analyzing the market by demographic characteristics.

Demographic characteristics can be used in developing products and targeting markets. For new customer acquisition, media buys and mailing lists can be aimed at households that have the specific demographic characteristics of the target market. Some firms have demographic data from the U.S. census appended to their customer file so that product development and direct-marketing efforts for existing customers can be more efficient.

Geodemographic Segmentation

Several national marketing firms have developed segmentation systems that divide the marketplace into distinct market segments based on census demographics of individual households and the geographic characteristics of where the household resides.

Geocoding is the process through which the geodemographic clusters are applied to a customer file. The geodemographic systems classify each of the 260,000 census block groups into a geodemographic cluster segment. A block group (or enumeration district in rural areas) is the smallest geographic limit for which the census reports complete data. It consists of 250 to 300 households. Since people have a tendency to naturally cluster in neighborhoods that reflect their lifestyles and socioeconomic status, these tend to be rather homogeneous units. Census blocks are determined through street addresses, and the predetermined cluster groups are then applied to the customer base.

Geodemographic segmentation systems divide the general population into segments, or clusters, based on similarities of socioeconomic and demographic variables. The demographics of a particular geographic unit (zip code, census tract, or block group) are reviewed, and then this unit is classified into one of the predefined segments.

This segmentation system can provide marketers with a more wholistic image of the target customer. In many cases a geodemographic segmentation system will incorporate such factors as age, income, home value and home ownership status into the segment or cluster definition.

An example of a geodemographic market segment is contained in Exhibit 3.3 on the following page. This segment is one of forty-eight diverse groups defined by National Decision Systems.

Financial institutions have successfully used geodemographic segmentation for both internal and external customer prospecting. Some firms have found strong correlations between certain geodemographic segments and response rates to particular product offerings.

Lifestyle Cluster Segmentation

Although demographic or geodemographic data is a powerful segmen-

Exhibit 3.3

Geodemographic Segment "Suburban Up and Comers"

Summary Profile

The last of the "baby boomers," these are the "full-nest" households and the "up and comers" in the new suburbs. They will become the "Tuition and Braces," "Nouveau Riche," and "Suburban Gentry" market segments in the 1990s. Very family oriented, they are predominantly white and thirty to forty-nine years old, with children and teens.

Clearly the well-educated, upper-middle class, almost seventy percent enjoy high income or better ($25,000 and up), and work primarily in managerial/ professional and technical/sales opportunities. Citizens of the new suburbs, 86% of their residences were built since 1960. This segment ranks number one in single unit housing and number two in property values from $80,000 to $150,000. Only nine percent are renters.

Demographic Profile

The heads of household are predominantly thirty to thirty-four (eight percent), thirty-five to thirty-nine (nine percent) and forty to forty-nine (sixteen percent) years old, with children (twenty percent) and teens (fifteen percent). The eleven percent that are fifty to fifty-nine years old are mostly "empty-nesters." The majority of this segment is white (ninety-two percent). Households of three to four people (forty-eight percent, 1.5 times the national average) and five or more (twenty-two percent, 1.6 times average) are the norm. Ranked No. 3 in average household size, this segment's average of 3.45 persons is higher than the U.S. average of 2.75.

Housing Profile

This segment ranks No. 1 in single unit residences (95%). Over 90% of households are owner occupied, and this segment ranks No. 2 in mid-high property values of $80,000 - $150,000 (Fifty-five percent fall in this category, nearly four times the average). More than two-thirds (sixty-nine percent) of the housing was built between 1960 and 1974, while another eighteen percent was built since 1974. Of the nine percent who rent, sixty-one percent pay high rent.

Location

This segment is eighty-four percent urban, with the highest concentration in

44

Hawaii (eight percent of the state's population and four times the national average). Other concentrations can be found in Maryland (six percent); Colorado and California (five percent each); New Jersey and Nevada (four percent each); and Connecticut, Arizona and Utah with three percent each.

Overall, this market segment represents 1.69 percent of all U.S. households.

Source: National Decision Systems VISION Marketing Guide, NDS, Encinitas, CA

Exhibit 3.4

Financial Lifestyle Segments

Market Segment	% of Market, Spring 1987
Service-assurance Seekers	9%
Trendy Credit Buyers	14%
Accumulator Leaders	13%
Ambitious, Security Driven	11%
People-oriented Traditionalists	16%
Institution Dependents	13%
Convenience Driven	10%
Price Alerts	14%

tation tool in the product development process it may not go far enough. Two people in the same demographic group probably have different opinions, habits, and buying patterns. Attitudes and values may explain why some individuals are excellent prospects and others with similar demographic characteristics are not.

Another type of segmentation research used for explaining these differences in buyer behavior is the examination of psychographic qualities, such as self-concept, interest, opinions, and other basic personality traits. Using this type of technique, the research can look at basic buying

EXHIBIT 3.5

Lifestyle Segment Synopsis

Service-assurance Seekers (9% of market)
- Smallest group
- Slightly younger than average
- Higher-than-average liquid balances
- Personal, friendly, fast, accurate, service important
- Rather spend a quiet evening at home than go out to a party

Trendy Credit Buyers (14% of market)
- Second-largest group
- Lowest liquid balances
- Average income
- Younger
- Spenders, not savers
- Heaviest users of unsecured credit

Accumulator Leaders (13% of market)
- Slightly older
- Higher income
- Average balances
- More likely to be white collar
- Traditional values, believe people are trustworthy, active leader in community, likes most people, better off financially over last year
- Best prospects for investment products

Ambitious, Security Driven (11% of market)
- Older than average
- Slightly lower-than-average income
- Higher liquid balances
- Family top priority, prefers quiet evenings at home, financial security very important
- Conservative investors

People-oriented Traditionalists (16% of market)
- Largest cluster group
- Oldest-on-average group
- Lowest average income
- Average balances
- Relies on financial institution for advice, feels it is important to be part of a group
- Personal service issues and image of financial institution very important
- Good CD usage

Institution Dependents (13% of market)
- Older than average
- Higher income
- Highest liquid balances
- Relies on financial institution for advice, financial security important

Convenience Driven (10% of market)
- Younger than average
- Lower-than-average income
- Lower-than-average balance
- Convenience issues most important (ATMs, drive-ins, hours, location)

Price Alerts (14% of market)
- Slightly younger than average
- Highest average income
- Second-highest balances
- Most-likely group to be white collar
- Willing to move for rate, uses more than one financial institution, wants to get ahead financially

styles, premium price preferences versus discounted prices, and life-style characteristics such as entertainment, travel, and community involvement. The market for financial services can be divided into groups or clusters of individuals who share similar attitudes toward managing their money and borrowing. By understanding lifestyle characteristics, product research can identify how a new or existing product should be positioned in the marketplace.

One example of a lifestyle segmentation system is the eight consumer market segments in the United States defined by the FIMA/Raddon National Research and shown in Exhibit 3.4.

The synopsis of the characteristics of these eight market segments in Exhibit 3.5 shows that certain preferences for products and services are more pronounced within some segments than in others. Knowing which segments will find a new idea for a product more appealing can be very helpful in developing positioning strategies for the product within a given market area.

By summarizing the demographics of these eight market segments, a financial institution can focus its product development research efforts on selected income and balance characteristics. Embellishing the infor-

Exhibit 3.6

Consumers' Financial Goals

Financial Goals	Total	Age of Consumer				
		18-34	35-44	45-54	55-64	65+
Increase retirement funds	68%	66%	76%	(81%)	73%	50%
Reduce taxes	60%	60%	71%	67%	69%	54%
Increase investments	60%	60%	67%	65%	60%	44%
Reduce outstanding debt	57%	(73%	66%)	51%	43%	21%
Balance monthly budget	48%	54%	54%	42%	42%	35%
Save for a child's education	44%	(62%	62%)	28%	12%	11%
Diversify investments	32%	32%	37%	38%	32%	21%
Purchase a home	27%	(47%)	28%	13%	11%	4%

Source: FIMA/Raddon National Research—Fall 1986

mation with lifestyle analysis and product utility heightens the probability of successful product development.

Remember, the basic purpose of market segmentation is to identify and locate more precisely the most-likely customer for a given product idea. The more information there is, the greater the likelihood of developing a message that will attract the attention of key market segments.

Consumer Needs Analysis

The ultimate objective of conducting research and employing a market segmentation plan is to gain an insight into consumers' needs so that a firm can efficiently develop products that address these needs and, at the same time, satisfy the firm's profit objectives.

Exhibit 3.7

Measuring Attractiveness of a New Product

As a result of deregulation, banks and savings associations will be expanding the list of services they can offer their customers. Which of the following services would you like to have available through your bank or savings association?

Service:	Percent of households wanting service:
Retirement counseling	55%
Tax-free mutual funds	42%
Tax-deferred annuities	40%
Insurance services	36%
Bond mutual funds	29%
Stock mutual funds	29%
Discount stock brokerage	27%
Full-service stock brokerage	23%

Source: FIMA/Raddon National Research—Fall 1985

One of the fundamental issues for product development is understanding consumers' financial goals. Exhibit 3.6 shows a list of financial goals cited by a national sample of consumers.

Research of this type points toward many product development and product positioning issues. To cite just few of these issues:

- Broaden IRA product-line offering and reposition as retirement planning

- Add tax-free mutual funds and tax-deferred annuities

- Position home-equity loans as an effective way to manage credit and reduce the cost of borrowing

- Offer a basic seminar, or handbook, on managing the family budget, setting goals, and using automatic payroll savings deductions

- Promote long-term, "double-or-triple-your-money" CDs as college fund builders

- Offer home-buyer seminars for younger customers

The attractiveness of new products can be quantified with basic concept testing as shown in Exhibit 3.7.

While the demand for these services is not quantified as explicitly as in the previous example on biweekly mortgage loans (Exhibit 3.2) some conclusions for product development priorities can still be drawn from these data.

Summary

The success of new products can be correlated to a strong commitment by a firm to monitor competition, internal strengths and weakness, and consumers' needs. Ideas for new products emerge from all of these sources of information.

A product evaluation matrix can be used for blending information gathered from management, staff, competitors, and consumers in a format that is conducive to establishing new product strategies.

Consumer focus groups can serve many purposes in the product development process. Focus groups provide the opportunity to explore new ideas, test concepts, and discover or validate processes.

There are several market research methodologies available for quantifying the demand for a new product or service including direct-mail consumer panels, telephone surveys, personal interviews, and competitive research. In general, quantitative research helps minimize the risks involved in offering new products.

Market segmentation allows a firm to divide the market into subgroups of homogeneous consumers with unique financial habits, buying pat-

tates the product development process by allowing an institution to customize features and to position a product to meet the needs of a particular market segment.

The ultimate objective of conducting research and employing a market segmentation plan is to gain an insight into consumers' needs so that a firm can efficiently develop products that address these needs and, at the same time, satisfy the firm's profit objectives.

Chapter 4

Product Analysis and Design

Product Planning and Management
Synchronization of Corporate Strategy
Competitive Positioning Assessment
Evaluation of Alternatives for a Product
Profit/Market Share Performance Analysis
The Product's Adoption Curve and Life Cycle
Product Line "Gap" Identification
Summary

Chapter 4

Product Analysis and Design

Product Planning and Management

Product planning and management opportunities are an outgrowth of the financial condition, market opportunities, and the composition of the customer base that is unique to each financial institution. The breadth of a product line offered by a financial institution should reflect the requirements necessary to meet the financial services needs of its targeted customer segments.

A financial institution should pragmatically focus its product development and management resources on two distinct product-line strategies. One strategy should be targeted toward increasing current customer profitability; and the second, targeted toward acquiring potentially profitable new customer relationships. Both strategies should be addressed concurrently in order to prevent financial and market-share growth performance objectives from becoming mutually exclusive.

The product development and management process requires the resolution of several marketing issues if they are to support the institution's strategic marketing objectives. These key marketing issues are: target market segment identification (Chapter 3), product profitability analysis (Chapter 5), pricing strategy execution (Chapter 6), and product promotion and communication (Chapter 7). The resolution of these issues, together with the issue of product design that is discussed in this chapter, ultimately comprises the product development and management process.

The product design and analysis process involves several different steps: synchronization with overall corporate strategic objectives, review of competitive positioning, evaluation of product alternatives, and analysis of profit and market-share performance potential. A product rollout plan is developed after management approves the product design and accepts the performance analysis projections.

Synchronization of Corporate Strategy

Decisions about product development are made within the context of the institution's overall competitive strategy. Competitive strategies fall into three general positioning categories: cost leadership, differentiation leadership, or targeted focus leadership.

Cost Leadership Positioning

This strategy pursues the achievement of the lowest delivered-cost position, combined with a pricing policy that produces profitable growth in volume, as well as in market share. Overall cost-leadership positioning is achieved through market-share dominance, vertical integration, efficient distribution systems, automation, technological superiority, or a combination of these. The overall strategic objective is to develop and/or retain a sustainable cost advantage in the products offered, or with the markets that the institution serves.

Differentiation Leadership Positioning

This strategy pursues the achievement of the highest product/service differentiation positioning relative to competitors. It is combined with a cost and pricing policy that produces sufficient profit margins to fund additional differentiation efforts. Overall differentiation positioning is generally based upon the prestige of the institution's name or products, product appeal, quality of service, and/or convenience advantages. The overall strategic objective is to develop and/or retain a sustainable perceived differentiation advantage in the products the institution offers or in the market that it serves.

Targeted Focus Leadership Positioning

This strategy pursues the domination of target market segments or specific product lines by creating cost- or differentiation-positioning advantages relative to competitors. The positioning advantages are derived from focusing on more specific market segments or product lines than do competitors. Overall, targeted focus leadership positioning still requires the achievement of a low-cost or differentiation advantage to be successful. However, the cost or differentiation advantage is focused on specific market segments or specific product lines. The strategic objective is to develop and/or retain significant competitive advantage within target market segments that the institution serves or specific products it offers.

Competitive Positioning Assessment

The competitive positioning assessment process should consider three areas: competitor strategies, current competitive pricing, and marketplace price-band sensitivity.

Competitor Strategies

Any analysis of primary competitors' product strategies should encompass their predisposition for introducing similar products in the past. Unless an institution has recently undergone a managerial or financial restructuring, a review of their past and current competitive actions provides a reasonable forecast of future competitive tendencies.

A competitor's anticipated response is often influenced by a variety of strategic constraints. Limitations of the data processing system's capacity, poor earnings performance, capital deficiencies, prior resource commitments, and organizational culture and structure are all potential constraints that can influence or limit a competitor's responses to another institution's product introduction.

Current Competitive Pricing

Institutions should, at least on a semiannual basis, compile a competitive pricing survey of their key competitors in the marketplace. Institutions should recognize that their key competitors may vary by product line. Their competition for residential and commercial mortgage loans for example, is not always going to be the same financial institution. Consumer deposit and commercial deposit competitors often vary. There probably exist numerous different combinations of key competitors for each group of financial services offered by an institution.

Marketplace Price-Band Sensitivity

On a weekly basis, institutions should track key competitors' interest rates and their own institution's internal funds flows for all rate-sensitive products. Product line performance trends should be tracked on a monthly, or at a minimum quarterly, basis to be matched with competitive marketplace promotional activities and events. All of these performance-trend indicators when combined with market research findings provide a picture of an institution's marketplace price sensitivity. This price-band concept is discussed in more detail in Chapter 6.

Evaluation of Alternatives for a Product

The evaluation of alternatives for a product is composed of three elements: What is the product's mission? What is the product offering strategy? What is the most effective tactical sales approach? The answers to these questions provide the product concept framework that guides the product development process.

The product concept framework starts with defining the product's mission. The product's mission is identified in terms of five customer status groups: potential customers, marginal customers, profitable customers, lucrative customers, and center-of-influence customers. Potential customers are prospective users of the product. Marginal customers are existing customers with either a limited and/or nonprofitable relationship that could be more advantageously restructured. Profitable customers are existing customers whose relationship with the institution should be expanded because of their untapped profit potential. Lucrative customers are customers whose relationship can be strengthened by a new product. Center-of-influence customers typically merit attention because of their access to other profitable business rather than their own business. Exhibit 4.1 shows the relationship between customer status and the product's mission. The identification of the product's mission directs the product's strategy.

Exhibit 4.1

Customer Status Group	Product Mission
Potential customer	Establish relationship
Marginal customer	Restructure relationship
Profitable customer	Expand or consolidate relationship
Lucrative customer	Protect relationship
Center-of-Influence customer	Leverage relationship

The product's strategy is driven by satisfying the financial service needs of the targeted segments within the customer group. The product's design matches the satisfaction of these financial services needs with the pricing offer, which in turn meets corporate objectives for financial and market-share performance. Exhibit 4.2 shows the range of pricing offers that shape a product's strategy.

Exhibit 4.2

Types of Pricing Offers

Attractiveness to the Financial Institution	Type of Pricing Offers	Tactical Examples of Pricing Offers
#1	Perceptual offer	a) Partial or full waiver of a credit policy requirement b) Access to group insurance services, purchasing power (i.e., club, auto, insurance) c) Merchant discount programs/coupons
#2	Related services offer	a) Installment loan interest rate discount b) Bonus interest rate % earnings c) "Free" services for maintaining another specified service relationship d) Checking service charge fee reductions
#3	Co-benefit offer	a) Completion insurance for IRAs or savings plans b) Disability insurance coverage
#4	Core service offer	a) Tier interest rate percent differentials for different deposit levels b) Renewal interest rate percentage bonuses or incentives for lengthening duration of their customer relationship c) Consumer credit interest payment discounts based upon level of outstanding loan balances
#5	Unrelated offer	a) Gift premiums b) AD&D common carrier insurance c) AD&D insurance coverage d) Club membership benefits

These are three basic tactical approaches to selling products and services within the financial industry: a product-intensive approach, a sales-system-intensive approach, and a people-intensive approach.

The product-intensive approach to selling financial services places the sales burden on the product itself. The product must be sufficiently appealing in terms of perceived benefits and/or price to sell itself. The primary promotion strategy is "pull-"oriented.

The sales-system-intensive approach relies on a heavy staff sales training commitment and an organizational sales culture. Sales results are achieved through sales-based compensation or special sales incentive programs. The primary promotion strategy is "push-"oriented.

The people-intensive approach relies on a relationship-building focus. Sales results are achieved through a combination of special service levels and relationship-banking product incentives. The promotion strategy is a combination of both "pull" and "push."

The selection of the tactical sales approach provides the final element of the concept for a product. Once management has approved the product's concept, the product development process is ready to move on to the product performance analysis.

Profit/Market Share Performance Analysis

The performance analysis for a potential product is a three stage process: product offer development, sales volume forecasting, and financial impact analysis. At each stage management's approval is needed before moving forward into the rollout stage of product development.

Product Offer Development

The product offering should be compatible and supportive of the institution's overall strategic positioning objectives. Its synergism with other product-line offerings of the institution is an important consideration. The product offer should be driven by the financial service needs of the target market segment(s).

The product's features and benefits should be fully supportable within the framework of legal requirements, human resource training resources, operation and data-processing implementation, corporate financial objectives, promotional strategy, and delivery system parameters.

Sales Volume Forecast

Sales volume forecasts are frequently missing in product development proposals, particularly when the product's concept has been initiated by or is in response to executive management's directives. The development of sales volume forecasts often requires resourceful gathering and interpretation of data—both internal institutional data and external market data.

Data used in the development of a sales volume forecast should be from a credible source or not utilized at all. Financial numbers should come from board reports, or approved financial budgets and plans. Market data should be developed from market research sources, established national data vendors (eg., Donnelley Marketing Services, BancPen, Sheshunoff, etc.), and trade association groups.

The data should be used to estimate different kinds of market opportunity: a market sales opportunity analysis, a sales forecast, and a gross income forecast. Exhibit 4.3 illustrates the conceptual process used to arrive at these estimates.

Market Sales Opportunity

The sales volume forecast incorporates a market opportunity analysis that projects the assumptions of marketplace demand for the product into sales and income potential. The following seven steps can be used to estimate market sales opportunity:

Step 1   Determine unit sales value

Step 2   Determine % of customer penetration =
Customer households/Total market area households

Step 3   Determine % of noncustomers =
(Total market area households-Customers households)
/Total market area households

Step 4   Determine overall product demand for customer households =
% Overall product demand x No. of customer households

Step 5   Determine overall product demand for noncustomer households =
% Overall product demand x No. of noncustomer households

EXHIBIT 4.3
MARKET OPPORTUNITY ANALYSIS MODEL FOR NON-TRADITIONAL FINANCIAL SERVICES

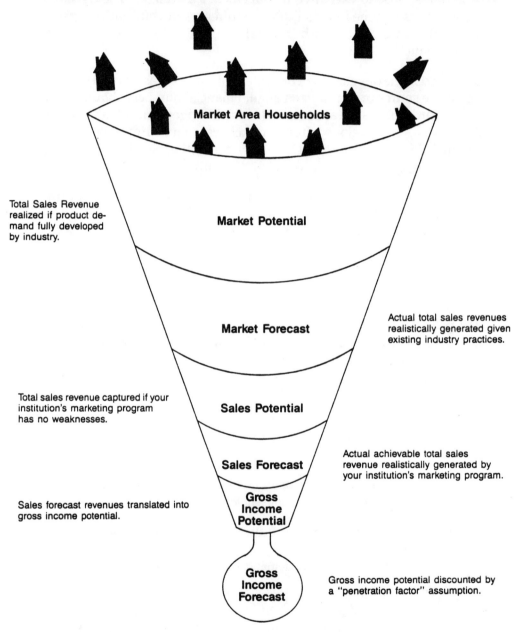

Market Area Households

Total Sales Revenue realized if product demand fully developed by industry.

Market Potential

Market Forecast

Actual total sales revenues realistically generated given existing industry practices.

Total sales revenue captured if your institution's marketing program has no weaknesses.

Sales Potential

Sales Forecast

Actual achievable total sales revenue realistically generated by your institution's marketing program.

Gross Income Potential

Sales forecast revenues translated into gross income potential.

Gross Income Forecast

Gross income potential discounted by a "penetration factor" assumption.

62

Step 6 Determine total market demand=
Overall product demand for customer households
+ Overall product demand for noncustomer households

Step 7 Market sales opportunity=
Unit sales value x Potential number of users

The following case study has been constructed to illustrate this process. An institution is contemplating offering a Convertible Mortgage product to its potential mortgage borrowers. National market research shows that 9% of all households will be taking out a mortgage loan within the next year. Exhibit 4.3a below shows the distribution of interest in a Convertible Mortgage among these households.

Exhibit 4.3a

Appeal of a Convertible Mortgage

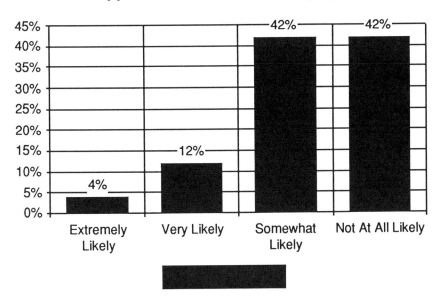

To provide meaningful interpretation of this national research data, the institution will have to apply it to its local market area. The institution must give consideration to the size of its market area, its penetration into the market, the potential among both customers and noncustomers in terms of overall mortgage demand, the appeal of a Convertible Mortgage, and the average purchase price for a home in its market area.

Product Analysis and Design

This information can be summarized as follows:

Unit Sales Value

Average home purchase price	$105,610
Downpayment @ 20%	$21,122
Total loan $ outstanding per potential borrowing HH	$84,488

Customer and Noncustomer Potential

	# of Total HHs	Customer HHs	Noncustomer HHs
% of market area HHs	100%	30%	70%
Market area HHs	200,000	60,000	140,000
Overall mortgage demand (@9%)	18,000	5,400	12,600
Demand for the product (@10%)	1,800	540	1,260
Market Sales Opportunity	$152,078,400	$45,623,520	$106,454,880

As seen above, the institution serves a market area of 200,000 households. The institution has established customer relationships with 30% of those households. National market research indicates 9% of those households will be taking out a mortgage loan within the next year. One can thus estimate that 5,400 of the institution's customers are potential mortgage borrowers. The same methodology can then be applied to noncustomer households.

National market research further shows that of those mortgage borrowers, 4% would be *extremely likely* to use a Convertible Mortgage product, while 12% would be *very likely* to use such a product. Considering that 1/2 of those very likely mortgage borrowers are not apt to act on their buying intentions, that leaves 6% of the very likely borrowers who would use the Convertible Mortgage product. The total demand for the product can therefore be estimated at 10% (4%+6%=10%). In terms of numbers, 540 customer households and 1,260 noncustomer households can be estimated to use the product.

Considering that the average purchase price for a home in this market is $105,610 and that the institution requires a 20% down payment, the potential Convertible Mortgage loan sales opportunity is $152 million. Given these relative measures, the institution should be able to determine the cost/benefit it may derive from proceeding in the development of this product.

From this estimate of market sales opportunity, a sales forecast can be derived. Forecasting techniques run from the more simplified and subjective use of methods such as jury of executive opinion (combining predictions from many key executives or salespeople in the firm to obtain a higher-quality estimate), to more sophisticated techniques like econometric forecasting. One of the most frequently used sales forecasting techniques, and one that would be appropriate in the case of a product line extension like the Convertible Mortgage, is some form of historical analysis, for example, time series analysis. Time series analysis is essentially the application of historical sales trends as a predictor of future sales.

Financial Impact Analysis

The financial impact analysis incorporates several steps: break-even analysis calculations, application of corporate-costing methodology, incorporation of unique product-feature costing, special promotional offer expenses, and the factoring of internal cannibalization or disintermediation.

The results of the financial impact analysis are combined with the earlier sales volume forecast data to construct a product profit proforma. Profit projections should cover a three-to-five year period to allow for the amortization of incremental customer acquisition costs that are associated with the product offer and to provide a clearer picture of the value of acquired customer relationships. The proforma should follow the traditional "conservative, most-likely, and optimistic" scenario format.

The final component of the financial impact analysis is the measurement of actual results. It is important to establish benchmark measurements for a product's performance prior to implementation. The product's rollout plan should incorporate a system for measuring the product's performance results. Measurement tools can be special product reports, research follow-up, or tracking of financial report data. Measurement of results is the key to improved product development and management capabilities.

The Product's Adoption Curve and Life Cycle

An institution's product-line development and management activities are influenced by two interrelated marketing concepts: the product's adoption curve and the product's life cycle. Exhibit 4.4 illustrates the concept of the "adoption curve." This marketing concept divides the

Product Analysis and Design

Exhibit 4.4

Product Adoption Curve

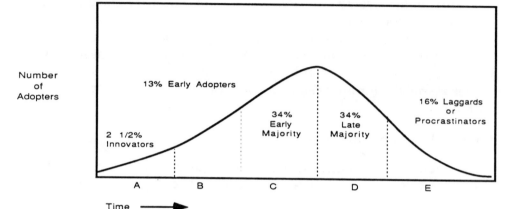

	Innovators	Early Adopters	Early Majority	Late Majority	Laggards or Procrastinators
Characteristics	Innovative	Aggressive	Trend follower	Conservative	Resistant to change
	First on the block	Second on the block	Imitators	Cautious	Last on the block
	Young & young thinking	Selectively innovative	No risk taking or innovation	Reluctant to change	Sure things only
	High mobility	Medium mobility	Low mobility	Little mobility	Almost zero mobility
	Global outlook & orientation	National outlook & orientation	Regional outlook & orientation	Local outlook & orientation	Individual outlook & orientation
	High prices O.K.	Prefer medium price but will pay high price	Prefer low price but will pay medium price	Bargain price driven	Closeout price oriented
"Hot Button" Terminology	Brand New	Successfully pilot tested	Well accepted	Proven for generations	Closeout
	Never before done	Be a leader	Widely used	Now on sale	Last of its kind
	Cutting edge	Jump on the bandwagon	Join the crowd	Special price	Below wholesale cost
	Most advanced yet	Still the most advanced	Improved	20 years of experience	Bankruptcy sale
	Be the first . . .	Only 1 out of 5 use	Successfully tried	Satisfaction guaranteed	Money back guarantee
	Trend setter	The choice of professionals	Most sold	70% of X use it	Lost lease
	Just introduced	As advertised in . . .	Sensibly priced tradition	New low price	Below cost
	Daring	New tradition	" . . . of the year" by well recognized magazine	Lowest price in town	Dealer sacrifice
	New era	Used by famous personalities	Endorsed by famous personalities	Get one free for trying	Clearance
	First time ever			Dependable/reliable	Going out of business
	New concept	Now available to public		Budget	Meet any price
	Avant garde	Introductory	Everybody wants	Giveaways	Won't be undersold
	Technological breakthrough	Limited time only	Used for X years	Best price ever	Free
	First of its kind				

66

Exhibit 4.5

Product/Services Portfolio
Lifecycle Analysis

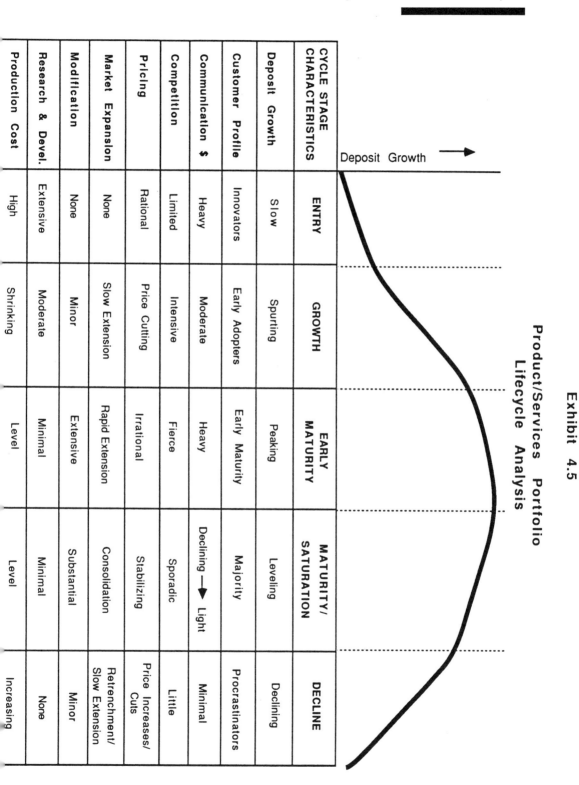

CYCLE STAGE CHARACTERISTICS	ENTRY	GROWTH	EARLY MATURITY	MATURITY/ SATURATION	DECLINE
Deposit Growth	Slow	Spurting	Peaking	Leveling	Declining
Customer Profile	Innovators	Early Adopters	Early Maturity	Majority	Procrastinators
Communication $	Heavy	Moderate	Heavy	Declining → Light	Minimal
Competition	Limited	Intensive	Fierce	Sporadic	Little
Pricing	Rational	Price Cutting	Irrational	Stabilizing	Price Increases/ Cuts
Market Expansion	None	Slow Extension	Rapid Extension	Consolidation	Retrenchment/ Slow Extension
Modification	None	Minor	Extensive	Substantial	Minor
Research & Devel.	Extensive	Moderate	Minimal	Minimal	None
Production Cost	High	Shrinking	Level	Level	Increasing

Deposit Growth →

universe of potential users of goods and services into five groups contingent upon their propensity to adopt a new product. These adoption characteristics correspond with the life cycle stages for product offers. The importance of understanding both concepts relates to their strategical and tactical implications for product development and management.

How well the institution's current customer base and target market segments correspond to the five adoption curve characteristics tells a great deal about the sales potential of a product and provides promotion and communication-positioning guidance for a product. Exhibit 4.4 also identifies personal characteristics and "hot-button" communication terminology associated with the five adoption curve market segments.

The concept of a product's life cycle looks at the same market picture from a product perspective rather than from a market segment perspective. All products progress through a life cycle, albeit at different speeds. The demand and profit potential remaining for a product is related to its position within this life cycle. The basic concept is that the demand and profitability growth for every product peaks at some point and begins an inevitable decline to a plateau or termination point, unless some external event or action extends or again recycles it.

Here again, the value of understanding the positioning of products in their life cycle stages provides valuable insight about what is presently happening to a product and what can be expected to happen in the future. Exhibit 4.5 shows various characteristics for the principal stages of a product's life cycle.

Product Line "Gap" Identification

Once the institution's market segmentation and competitive-positioning assessment processes are complete, current product development needs and priorities should be apparent. A market segment and product/services needs matrix readily identifies the product line "design gaps" that the institution needs to eliminate. These product line gaps can be addressed by either repositioning existing products or by developing new products.

Financial institutions can categorize their products/services into at least four broad groups. The labeling of these groups may differ, but the principle and process are always applicable. Exhibit 4.6 provides a model matrix format for this analysis process.

Exhibit 4.6

Product Line Gap Identification

Market Segment Type	Transaction Prod./Serv.	Savings/Investment Prod./Serv.	Credit Prod./Serv.	Retirement/Security Prod./Serv.
List each of your institution's target market types.		NOTE: List current products that have market appeal to each specific segment type. Also list product design gaps (either no product or current products lack market segment appeal).		

Once the product lines design gaps are identified, the product's needs are prioritized relative to resource requirements for development and opportunities for profit. Exhibit 4.7 provides an example of this prioritization evaluation. Most institutions find the prioritization process necessary because of limitations in promotional resources rather than in operational, sales, or delivery constraints.

Summary

Financial institutions should concurrently focus product development and management resources on increasing the profitability of current customers and on acquiring new customer relationships. Recognition of the existence of these two distinctive product line strategies allows financial institutions to concurrently pursue financial and market-share growth performance objectives.

The first step in the product design and analysis process involves synchronization of product development decisions with the overall corporate competitive strategy. Competitive strategies typically revolve around the achievement of cost leadership, differentiation leader-

EXHIBIT 4.7
PRODUCT/SERVICES OPPORTUNITY EVALUATION

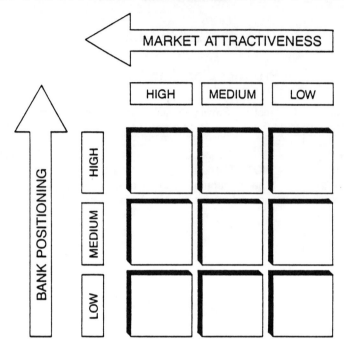

KEY: (H = High; M = Medium; L = Low)

Factor	Market Attractiveness	Bank Position	Factor	Market Attractiveness	Bank Position
1. Market Size			13. Skills Fit		
2. Market Growth			14. Product Synergism		
3. Segmentation Ease			15. Cyclical Synergism		
4. Penetration Cost			16. Profit Margins		
5. Market Share			17. Image Fit		
6. Defensive Motivation			18. Differentia- tion		
7. Entry Requirements			19. Capital Resources		
8. Competitive Climate			20. People Resources		
9. Regulatory/ Social Climate			21. Price Sensitivity		
10. Distribution System			22. On-Stream Time		
11. Systems/ Tech Barriers			23. Critical Volume		
12. Capacity			24. Entry		

70

ship, or a targeted focus leadership positioning advantages. Product development and management activities support the institution's efforts to develop and/or sustain the cost, perceived differentiation, or competitive target market segment/specific product advantages appropriate for its corporate strategy.

An institution's competitive-positioning assessment encompasses competitive strategies, current competitive pricing, and marketplace price-band sensitivity. Competitors' tendencies, strategic constraints, pricing tactics, and the price-band sensitivity of the target segments in the marketplace are key aspects of the competitive evaluation process.

The evaluation of alternatives for a product includes the definition of the product's mission, offering strategy, and most-effective sales tactics. A product's mission is identified in terms of acquiring, restructuring, deepening, strengthening, or leveraging of customer relationships. The product-offering strategy is driven by satisfying the financial service needs of targeted customers. Promotional approaches are premised upon the sales-pulling power of the product's design, the sales-pushing power of the sales channels, or the relationship-building strength of the quality of service.

Product performance analysis involves the product offer development, sales volume forecast, and financial impact analysis. The product offer development design assures conformance with corporate strategic-positioning objectives, satisfying the financial service needs of targeted customers, and compatibility with corporate resources. The sales volume forecast incorporates a market opportunity analysis that projects the assumptions of the product's marketplace demand into sales and income potential. The financial impact analysis quantifies the sales and income potential in terms of financial performance measurement benchmarks.

Product development and management strategically reflect the product adoption curve and product life cycle marketing concepts. The product's adoption curve indicates sales potential and provides product promotion/communication guidance from a market segmentation perspective. The product's life cycle indicates sales demand and profit potential from a product usage perspective. Understanding these concepts as they relate to a specific product development or management activity provides valuable insight about a product's future potential.

The completion of the market segmentation and competitive-positioning processes should identify the product-line gaps to be addressed by product development activities. Product needs should be prioritized relative to their developmental resource requirements and the opportunity for profit. Each financial institution should determine its own criteria in evaluating priorities for comparative product development.

Chapter 5

Product Profitability Measurement Tools

Account Profitability—A Few Considerations
Measuring Relationship Profitability—The Affect ofTechnology
Measuring Account Profitability—
The Federal Reserve's Functional Cost Analysis Program
The "Breakeven Analysis" Concept
Measuring Financial Relationship Profitability
Measuring Market Segment Profitability
Issue: Market Segmentation Profitability
Summary

Chapter 5

Product Profitability Measurement Tools

For years the business of banking was rather straightforward and simple. It involved taking fairly abundant but low-cost deposits and investing them in loans and other investments at yields sufficient to generate the necessary margins required to cover all operating costs and return a profit.

However, the entrance of totally deregulated rates into the competitive framework has created a different environment. With rate as a competitive factor, all accounts are subject to pricing decisions and are vulnerable to competitors paying a higher rate, especially when introducing a new product.

Account Profitability—A Few Considerations

The profitability of any account depends upon four factors:

- The cost incurred by the institution for maintaining the account

- The level of balances maintained in the account

- The rate spread between the sources and uses of those balances

- Explicit fees levied on the account

Measuring Relationship Profitability— The Affect of Technology

New technology in data processing has provided the tools for identifying multiple accounts held by one individual or by many individuals living in the same household. The marketing customer information file (MCIF) makes it possible to understand both multiple relationships held by one household and the profitability of the entire relationship.

━━━━━━━━

The rest of this chapter will focus on how to estimate the profitability of an individual deposit account. How multiple account relationships contribute to profitability will then be examined. Finally, segmentation, product usage, and balances will be studied together to determine the profitability potential of market segments based on lifestyle, age and income.

Measuring Account Profitability—
The Federal Reserve's
Functional Cost Analysis (FCA) Program

The Functional Cost Analysis (FCA) program is a cooperative venture between the Federal Reserve Banks and the participating banks and savings institutions. With uniform reporting procedures, it is designed to serve as a tool for financial institution's management in evaluating performance.

The FCA develops individual institution data on income and cost along functional lines and provides comparisons of these data within each institution from year to year and with groups of other banks on an annual basis. It is specifically designed to assist a participating institution in increasing overall earnings, as well as improving the operational efficiency of each function.

Functional cost data on a national basis can be used for comparing a financial institution's own costs. Costs are broken down into overhead allocation and direct costs associated with originating and maintaining a product.

Data are collected for commercial banks and savings institutions. Separate reports are furnished for each type of institution. In 1985, 504 commercial banks and 96 savings institutions participated in the study. These data are then broken out by size of institution.

There are some limitations that should be noted when using functional cost data. The data reflects averages from surveyed institutions, and there can be significant variation between institutions in the average cost of an item. Functional cost is a diagnostic and analytical tool to be used only as one aspect for making pricing decisions—other information is required as well. Finally, the small number of savings institutions participating in the program makes it difficult for a savings institution to draw general conclusions from the data.

Exhibits 5.1 through 5.4 are examples of cost data from four products included in the 1985 functional cost data for savings institutions. The cost data are broken down for institutions of three deposit sizes: under $50 million, $50 million to $200 million, and over $200 million.

Exhibit 5.1

Interest Bearing Checking Account

Activity Costs

	Size of Institution		
	Up to $50mm	$50mm to $200mm	Over $200mm
On-Us Debits	$0.19	$0.15	$0.23
Deposits	0.36	0.30	0.49
Transit Checks	0.11	0.08	0.13
Account Maintenance	4.27	3.98	6.64

1985 Thrift Functional Cost Analysis—Page 13

Note: Includes NOW Accounts and other checking accounts on which the institution is paying interest.

Product Profitability Measurement Tools

EXHIBIT 5.2

Regular Savings Accounts

NOTE: Includes Regular Savings Only.

Activity Costs

	Up to $50mm	$50mm to $200mm	Over $200mm
Deposits	$0.23	$0.42	$0.70
Withdrawals	$0.45	$0.81	$1.36
Account Opened (Amortized)	$1.42	$2.56	$4.30
Account Closed (Amortized)	$0.78	$1.40	$2.36
Interest Postings	$0.88	$1.58	$2.56
Annual Account Maintenance	$5.97	$10.72	$18.03

1985 Thrift FCA-Page 18

EXHIBIT 5.3

Certificates Of Deposit Under $100,000

Annual Expense

	Up to $50mm	$50mm to $200mm	Over $200mm
Account Opening	$1.06	$1.91	$3.21
Account Closed	$0.94	$1.70	$2.86
Interest Payments	$0.80	$1.44	$2.43
Annual Account Maintenance	$1.40	$2.51	$4.23

1985 Thrift Functional Cost Analysis—Page 18

EXHIBIT 5.4

Installment Loan Function

	Up to $50mm	$50mm to $200mm	Over $200mm
Number of Loans Outstanding	5,349	4,865	10,406
Total Loan Volume ($000)	16,975	17,920	46,466
Loan Volume Mix:			
Consumer Installment Loan	93.48%	85.98%	57.12%
Check Credit Loans	3.90%	4.38%	5.56%
Commercial Equipment and Other Loans	2.61%	9.45%	37.11%
Floor Plan	-	.18%	.19%
	100%	100%	100%
Expense: *(as a % of outstandings)*			
Salaries and Fringe	1.28%	1.25%	1.49%
Total Operating Expense	2.66%	2.51%	3.07%
Three Year Average - Loan Losses	0.31%	0.35%	0.19%
Total Personnel (# on staff)	9.59%	11.05%	32.22%
Miscellaneous Data:			
Average Size Loan	$3,173	$3,683	$4,465
Number of Applicants Processed	5,419	3,121	6,098
Loans Made % of Applicants	80.87%	86.13%	79.22%
Number Loans Made	4,383	2,688	4,831
Production Data:			
Volume of Loans/Officer ($000)	$6,603	$6,470	$6,913
Loans Made/Officer	1,704	970	718
Loans Outstanding/Person	557	440	322
Applications Processed/Person	564	282	189
Loans Made/Person	456	243	149

1985 Thrift Functional Cost Analysis—Pages 27 and 28

The "Breakeven Analysis" Concept

Internal or external cost data can be used to aid pricing decisions in several ways. One application is the creation of breakeven average-balance requirements from which minimum-balance pricing requirements for deposit products can be set. In determining breakeven balances, the revenues and costs associated with each product must be isolated.

The two potential sources of revenue are:

- Earnings from balances
- Explicit fees

With checking accounts, NOW accounts, and SuperNOW accounts, the concept of charging fees and/or paying less interest on low-balance accounts is well established. But with savings accounts, the concept is fairly new. Conceptually, the idea of charging explicit fees on low-balance savings accounts has a great deal of merit. Consumers are provided a valuable service when they keep their money in the bank (i.e. safekeeping, record keeping, and insurance), and it is logical that they should pay for this "savings" service in either fees or balances.

To properly price transaction, savings, and investment accounts, the concept of net-interest margin or spread must be understood.

Net-Interest Margin

The net-interest margin is the value to the institution of depositors' money as it is invested in loans and other investments. It is computed by taking the asset yield and subtracting the interest costs. It is analogous to a retail store's gross margin, in that with it the institution must pay all salaries, occupancy overhead, and other expenses plus return a profit to the financial institution.

The net-interest margin is the source of all cost recovery and profit to an institution, and it determines the breakeven balance level for each of the various sources of funds. An institution's net-interest is determined by two variables:

- The institution's yield on earning assets
- Its asset mix

Determining Asset Yield

Traditionally, for example savings and loans and mutual savings banks have invested the bulk of their core deposits into mortgages. However, with the new asset powers, future deposits may eventually go into each of the following "use-of-funds" categories, plus perhaps others.

- Investment portfolio

- Real estate loans

- Installment loans

- Commercial loans

To simplify this analysis, make the assumption that each dollar of core deposits will be allocated to the "earnings-asset portfolio" according to a mix of assets. The question then becomes:

What is the average yield on earning assets?

The answer is a function of two things:

- Yields on various assets

- Asset mix

Gross Yield vs. "Yield-After-Operating-Costs"

Just as FCA studies show that there are operating costs associated with acquiring deposits, so there are operating costs associated with using funds. In other words, when a loan is made costs are incurred such as: the salary of the loan officer and credit analyst, the credit application and analysis procedure, developing the loan contract, and the loss on bad loans. These costs must come out of the potential income stream of the loan before the resultant yield-after-operating-costs can be used to determine the profitability of deposits (i.e. source-of-funds).

To determine the asset yield, a look at a savings institution's yield on various assets and the mix of these will prove helpful. The FCA reveals the following gross yields, operating costs, and asset mix for firms having between $50 million and $200 million in deposits as of 1985 (see Exhibit 5.5a).

This average net yield can be adjusted to reflect an institution's current portfolio. The higher the average net yield, the fewer balances will be

Exhibit 5.5a

Average Net Yield

Use of Funds	Gross Yield	Acquisition & Operating Costs	Net Yield	% of Earning Assets	Weighted Average* Yield Factor
Investments	10.00%	0.229%	9.771%	36.71%	3.00%
Real estate	11.07%	0.739%	10.335%	50.82%	5.25%
Installment	13.22%	3.060%	10.162%	14.19%	1.44%
Credit card	17.52%	12.06%	5.45%	0.20%	0.01%
Commercial	12.20%	2.18%	10.02%	4.04%	0.40%
				Average net yield =	10.10%

Figures used are 1985 FCA data for interest-bearing transaction accounts.

*Net Yield x % of Earning Assets = Weighted Average

needed to pay the cost of servicing the account; and, conversely, the lower the asset yield, the higher the balance level needed to pay for the cost of carrying the account.

Breakeven Deposit Sizes

The information given above provides all the data that is needed to determine the minimum economic deposit size for each category of deposits. The breakeven computation is as follows:

$$\frac{\text{Annualized Deposit Operating Costs}}{(\text{Net Yield- Interest Rate On Deposits}) \times (1.00) - \text{Float}} = \text{Breakeven Balance}$$

Exhibit 5.5b shows that the breakeven average balance for interest checking at a medium-size savings institution is $3,353. Assuming that customers will hold an average account balance that is twice the minimum balance, an institution would have to require a minimum balance of $1,676 to breakeven on interest-bearing accounts. This analysis does

The "Breakeven Analysis" Concept

<hr>

EXHIBIT 5.5b

Breakeven Analysis - NOW Account

Earnings Credit on NOW Account Balances

Earning Asset Yield x Float and Reserve Adjustment

10.10 x .78   =   7.88%

Interest Rate Paid on NOW Balances   <u>5.25%</u>

Net Earnings Credit on NOW Balances   =   2.63%

Fixed Monthly Maintenance Cost	=	$3.98
Variable Costs:		
Per Check	=	$0.15
Per Deposit	=	$0.30
Per Transit Check	=	<u>$0.08</u>

Total Annual Costs Per Account   = $88.20

Breakeven Annual Balance   =   <u>$88.20</u> (3)

                              2.63% (2)   = $3,353

Breakeven Minimum Balance   = $1,676

National averages. . . 1985 Functional Cost Analysis. . . Savings Institutions $50mm-$200mm

Product Profitability Measurement Tools

EXHIBIT 5.6

BREAKEVEN ANALYSIS - REGULAR SAVINGS

Earnings Credit on Savings Balances

    Earning Asset Yield x Float Adjustment

        10.10 x .9953   =   10.03%

    Interest Expense   =   5.62%

    Net Earnings Credit   =   4.41%

Costs Per Account

    Fixed Annual Maintenance Cost   = $10.72

    Variable Costs:

        Per Deposit   = $0.42

        Per Withdrawal   = $0.81

        Amortized Opening and Closing Costs   = $0.61

        Interest Postings   = $1.58

Annual Activity*

    Maintenance   =   1.0

    Deposits   =   13.5

    Withdrawals   =   8.4

    Amortized Opening and Closing   =   1.0

    Interest Postings   =   8.0

Total Annual Cost Per Account

    Maintenance Cost   = $10.72

    Variable Costs:

        Deposits   = $5.67

        Withdrawals   = $6.80

        Amortized Opening and Closing   = $0.61

        Interest Posting   =   <u>$12.64</u>

                                            $36.44

Breakeven Average Balance $\dfrac{\$36.44}{4.41\%}$ = $826

National averages. . . 1985 Functional Cost Analysis. . . Savings Institutions $50mm-$200mm

not account for any fee-income that the institution would receive for customers going below the minimum, margin on check orders, NSF, and stop payments. Estimates of these explicit fees must also be factored in before an actual profitability estimate can be determined.

Exhibit 5.6 presents the breakeven average balance ($826) on a regular savings account that pays a compounded yield of 5.62 percent and costs $36.44 per year.

Measuring Financial Relationship Profitability

Using the breakeven computation as a tool for understanding the costs and profitability of an individual account makes it possible to move one step further toward evaluating household-relationship profitability.

The movement of the early 1980s was toward making each individual account profitable on a stand-alone basis. Many pricing practitioners felt that higher-balance accounts had for too long subsidized low-balance unprofitable accounts. Some repricing moves resulted in a loss of high-balance profitable relationships, as customers holding high-balance profitable accounts reacted angrily to service fee increases on their lower-balance "convenience" accounts.

Typically, 20 percent of customer households provide 80 percent of deposit dollars. The "80/20 rule" is found consistently in both savings institutions and commercial banks.

Marketing customer information files (MCIFs) make it possible for an institution to tie together all of the accounts in a customer's household in order to examine the customer's relationship with the institution as he or she views it. The majority of MCIFs currently in use are not tied to the day-to-day operational systems of financial institutions. They are analytical tools that assist institutions in many ways. However, they rarely allow an institution to establish a relationship pricing policy that rewards or penalizes a customer or household based upon the total profitability of the entire relationship. The next wave of technology will probably provide that important ability. For now, the analytical abilities of financial institutions are being challenged to maximize the value of currently available technology.

Exhibits 5.7 and 5.8 show the household balance distribution of a savings institution. Note that of the institution's 50,606 households, 11,475 (or 22.6%) contribute 80.1 percent of total deposits.

EXHIBIT 5.7

SAMPLE DISTRIBUTION

DEPOSIT HOUSEHOLD
BALANCE DISTRIBUTION

Household Balance Range	Total Households	Percent Household (Cumulative)	Percent of Total	Total Balances	Percent Balances (Cumulative)	Percent of Total
$ Negative	1	.0%	.0%	($54)	0.0%	0.0%
$ Zero Balance	409	0.8%	0.8%	0	0.0%	0.0%
$.01-100	3,616	8.0%	7.1%	140,275	0.0	0.0%
$101-500	5,409	18.6%	10.7%	1,409,673	0.2%	0.2%
$501-1,000	4,724	28.0%	9.3%	3,430,313	0.6%	0.4%
$1,001-5,000	13,270	54.2%	26.2%	33,368,348	4.6%	4.0%
$5,001-10,000	5,688	65.4%	11.2%	40,770,709	9.5%	4.9%
$10,001-20,000	6,014	77.3%	11.9%	86,124,893	19.9%	10.4%
$20,001-100,000	10,341	97.8%	20.4%	462,507,822	75.6%	55.7%
Over $100,000	1,134	100.0%	2.2%	202,755,402	100.0%	24.4%
Total	50,606		22.6%	$830,507,380		80.1%

NOAH Banking Services - Omaha, Nebraska

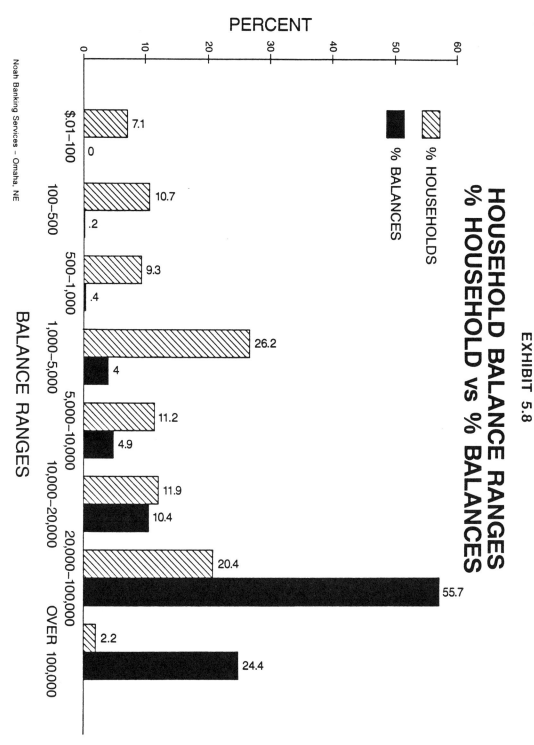

EXHIBIT 5.8

HOUSEHOLD BALANCE RANGES
% HOUSEHOLD vs % BALANCES

Noah Banking Services – Omaha, NE

87

Product Profitability Measurement Tools

EXHIBIT 5.9

Single Service Households

Product	% of Total Service Households	% of Total Service Balances	% of Total Household Balances	Average Household Balance
Checking	46.5%	36.2%	3.3%	$ 3,873
Savings	62.8%	38.9%	4.9%	$ 2,495
Money Market	36.1%	35.2%	9.2%	$20,795
Retirement	36.6%	30.0%	1.9%	$ 6,869
Certificate	47.5%	47.0%	21.5%	$27,601
Total	70.9%		40.8%	$ 9,448

EXHIBIT 5.10

Dual Service Households

Product	% of Total Service Households	% of Total Service Balances	% of Total Household Balances	Average Household Balance
Checking	32.2%	45.9%	13.3%	$22,166
Savings	23.6%	43.5%	17.8%	$24,094
Money Market	33.8%	33.5%	13.7%	$33,352
Retirement	25.6%	26.2%	4.4%	$22,631
Certificate	30.0%	29.9%	18.4%	$37,325
Total	20.0%		33.8%	$27,746

Exhibit 5.9 shows the percentage of households that use only one type of service with the institution. Seven out of ten (70.9%) customers households use only one type of service. These single-service households account for 40.8 percent of the institution's total deposits, with an average household balance of $9,448.

These customers provide an important target audience for the institution's new product development efforts. An MCIF can provide additional insight into the demographics of this customer segment, thereby further enhancing the new product development process.

Increasing the number of services held by any customer is important because the more services a customer obtains from an institution, the less likely he or she is to sever his or her relationship with the institution.

Exhibit 5.10 shows that 20 percent of households use two services with the institution. These households have an average household balance of $27,746, and account for 33.8 percent of the total deposits.

Exhibit 5.11 shows that households using more than one service exceed single-service households with every type of deposit product except savings.

Exhibit 5.12 indicates the average household deposits for different levels of service usage. Households using over three services have an average deposit balance of $61,896.

Exhibit 5.13 combines related data and functional cost data to determine account profitability on an individual account, as well as, on a household-relationship basis.

In this institution's case, the NOW account shows a total loss of $411,170 when evaluated on a stand-alone basis. Profit contributions from related accounts add about $3.8 million in income to NOW account households, bringing total household profit from NOWs and related accounts to $350.44 per household.

At this level of analysis, the institution can understand the overall profit contribution of checking account households. As MCIF technology develops, institutions will be able to implement pricing techniques that identify and reward profitable households, while charging a service fee to those households that do not contribute a profit to the institution. In addition, institutions will be able to cross-sell appropriate services to less profitable households.

EXHIBIT 5.11

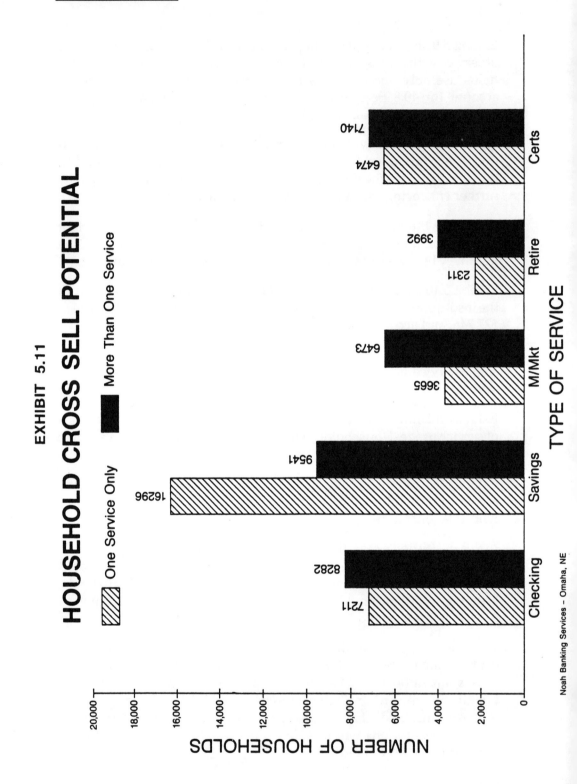

HOUSEHOLD CROSS SELL POTENTIAL

One Service Only

More Than One Service

NUMBER OF HOUSEHOLDS

TYPE OF SERVICE

Checking: 7211, 8282
Savings: 16296, 9541
M/Mkt: 3665, 6473
Retire: 2311, 3992
Certs: 6474, 7140

Noah Banking Services – Omaha, NE

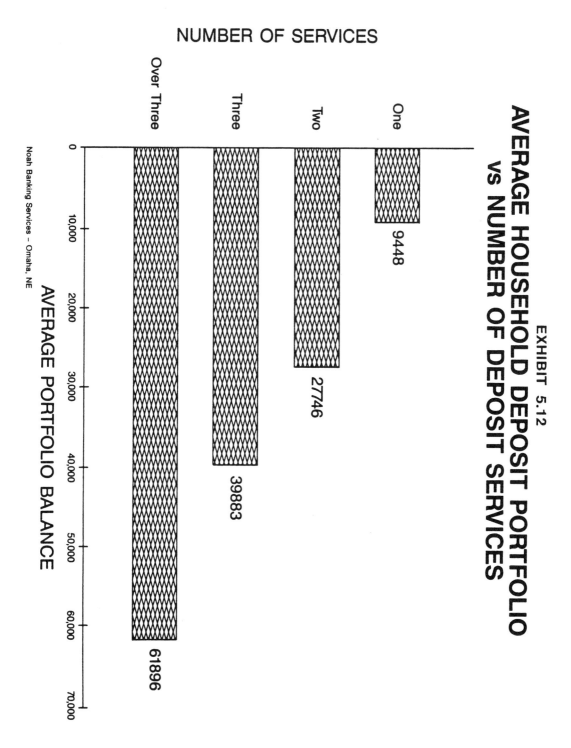

NUMBER OF SERVICES

AVERAGE HOUSEHOLD DEPOSIT PORTFOLIO
vs NUMBER OF DEPOSIT SERVICES

EXHIBIT 5.12

AVERAGE PORTFOLIO BALANCE

Noah Banking Services – Omaha, NE

One — 9448

Two — 27746

Three — 39883

Over Three — 61896

EXHIBIT 5.13

CUSTOMER RELATIONSHIP MATRIX

NOW Accounts	Total NOWs	Related Savings	Related MMA	Related CDS	Related CDL	Related IRA
Percent	100.00%	22.72%	30.80%	12.72%	11.87%	3.04%
Number	10,774	2,448	3,318	1,370	1,279	328
Avg. Balance	$1,537	$2,120	$10,594	$25,752	$26,667	$7,561
Total Balances	$16,559,638	$5,189,760	$35,150,892	$35,280,240	$34,107,093	$2,480,008
% of Balances Invested	90.81%	99.53%	99.53%	99.53%	99.53%	99.53%
Portfolio Yield	9.75%	9.75%	9.75%	9.75%	9.75%	9.75%
Portfolio Income	$1,466,186	$503,623	$3,411,104	$3,423,656	$3,309,812	$240,664
Cost of Funds	5.37%	5.68%	5.68%	7.39%	8.90%	7.52%
Interest Expense	$889,253	$294,778	$1,996,571	$2,607,210	$3,035,531	$186,497
Non-int. Cost per Acct.	$111.69	$53.48	$63.39	$15.77	$6.02	$41.79
Operating Costs	$1,203,348	$130,919	$210,328	$21,605	$7,700	$13,707
Total Serv. Chg. Income	$215,244					
****Total Profit****	($411,170)	$77,926	$1,204,205	$794,842	$266,581	$40,461
Profit per Account	($38.16)	$31.83	$362.93	$580.18	$208.43	$123.36

	Related ISL	Related LOC	Related JUM	Related CCA	Related MOR	TOTALS
Percent	1.64%	2.66%	0.30%	11.52%	13.53%	
Number	177	287	32	1,241	1,458	22,712
Avg. Balance	$5,352	$27,678	$133,033	$627	$48,145	
Total Balances	$947,304	$7,943,586	$4,257,056	$778,107	$70,195,410	$212,889,094
% of Balances Invested	99.53%	99.53%	99.53%	99.53%	100.00%	
Portfolio Yield	14.80%	10.75%	9.75%	15.00%	9.75%	
Portfolio Income	$139,542	$849,922	$413,112	$116,167	$6,844,052	$20,717,842
Cost of Funds	7.37%	7.37%	7.44%	7.37%	7.37%	
Interest Expense	$69,816	$585,442	$316,725	$57,346	$5,173,402	$15,212,571
Non-int. Cost per Acct.	$168.00	$96.00	$11.42	$6.46	$200.00	
Operating Costs	$29,736	$27,552	$365	$8,017	$291,600	$1,944,877
Total Serv. Chg. Income						$215,244
****Total Profit****	$39,990	$236,928	$96,022	$50,804	$1,379,051	$3,775,638
Profit per Account	$225.93	$825.53	$3,000.68	$40.94	$945.85	$350.44

Measuring Market Segment Profitability

With an understanding of how to measure profit on both an account and a relationship basis, marketing efforts can be adjusted to target segments that will provide an opportunity for profit on a household-relationship basis.

This section details product usage data and balance data for various demographic and lifestyle market segments. The data is from a national research sample of 1,022 households conducted by the Raddon Financial Group in March 1987. The sample is balanced to represent all regions of the country. The data on product usage and balances maintained is combined with Federal Reserve Functional Cost Data to calculate the

Exhibit 5.14

Checking Account Usage

Demographics	Regular % With	Regular Average Balance	Interest-Bearing % With	Interest-Bearing Avarage Balance	Market Rate % With	Market Rate Average Balance*
Total	48%	$929	39%	$3,155	6%	$13,077
Liquid assets						
Less than $10K	56%	644	35%	1,164	2%	5,400
$10K-$25K	45%	967	43%	2,898	8%	4,718
$25K or more	40%	1,424	46%	6,355	11%	13,968
Income						
Less than $25K	50%	698	37%	2,749	3%	5,427
$25K-$50K	48%	913	43%	2,970	6%	10,080
$50K or more	40%	1,548	44%	4,671	14%	20,285
Age						
18-34	49%	763	41%	1,234	5%	5,419
35-44	52%	801	37%	1,607	7%	9,565
45-54	51%	770	40%	2,237	5%	12,600
55-64	46%	1,015	40%	3,191	6%	8,100
65+	45%	1,368	41%	7,373	7%	11,484

*Small sample size in some cases.

Exhibit 5.15

Value of the Primary Relationship

	Average Household Total Deposits	Percent at Primary Institution	$ at Primary Instition
Total	$23,524	60%	$14,114
Liquid assets			
Less than $10K	4,581	63%	2,886
$10K-$25K	17,225	56%	9,648
$25K or more	59,352	59%	35,018
Income			
Less than $25K	15,545	63%	9,794
$25K-$50K	22,473	61%	13,708
$50K or more	46,396	52%	24,126
Age			
18-34	8,645	64%	5,532
35-44	13,819	60%	8,291
45-54	22,693	60%	13,616
55-64	33,116	56%	18,555
65+	42,907	62%	26,602

average profit contribution to the industry from the various market segments.

This powerful tool provides an understanding of where the greatest opportunities for profit exist, as well as what products and services create that profit. Product development should focus on the opportunities for profit afforded by key market segments. The objective should be to maximizing total relationship profitability by having the right combination of services available.

Exhibit 5.14 shows the usage of various types of checking accounts. Regular checking is still the dominant primary relationship account. However, interest-bearing and market-rate checking are growing faster

Exhibit 5.16

Checking Usage—Main Account Balances

	Regular		Interest-Bearing		Market Rate	
	% With	Average Balance	% With	Average Balance	% With	Average Balance
Total	48%	$929	39%	$3,155	6%	$13,077
Service-assurance Seekers	45%	590	40%	3,574	9%	19,214
Trendy Credit Buyers	54%	815	39%	1,777	1%	1,170
Accumulator Leaders	51%	1,087	38%	2,497	10%	11,372
Security Driven	47%	1,384	43%	2,898	6%	8,131
Traditionalists	43%	1,047	36%	4,424	5%	3,839
Institution Dependents	47%	853	41%	5,630	8%	15,449
Convenience Driven	55%	778	39%	2,332	-	-
Price Alerts	44%	860	42%	2,316	10%	9,360

than no-interest checking. The targeted markets are high-income and high-balance households, the best results are achieved by offering an interest-bearing checking account. Age is not a significant indicator of the type of checking account used. However, older customers maintain higher balances in all types of accounts compared with other age groups.

In Exhibit 5.15, consumers were asked what percent of their total deposits they keep at their primary financial institution. The average household has $23,524 in deposits and keeps 60 percent of these deposits at the primary financial institution. Capturing the customer's primary relationship is of great value to an institution because the institution then is more likely to successfully solicit the next deposits. For example, the low-income households, on average, keep 63 percent of their deposits at their primary financial institution. Middle-income households keep a slightly lower percentage of funds at their primary institution, yet their deposits are substantially higher.

Secondary financial institutions may have up to $4 of every $10, or 40 percent of what a household possesses. The strategy of secondary financial institutions should be to gain as much of the other 60 percent as possible. At some point the secondary institution may even have an opportunity to become the customer's primary financial institution.

Exhibit 5.16 shows the usage of various types of checking accounts by households segmented on the basis of lifestyle. A description of each of these lifestyle segments is provided in Chapter 3. The growing appeal of interest and market-rate checking is now equal to or greater than the appeal of non-interest checking among the following market segments: Service-assurance Seekers, Security Driven, Institution Dependents, and Price Alerts. Segments to target for profitable relationships are the Service-assurance Seekers, the Traditionalists, and the Institution Dependents.

Exhibit 5.17

Product Usage—Balances

	Passbook			Statement Savings		
	% With Product	Average Balance	% 5K+	% With Product	Average Balance	% 5K+
Total	55%	$4,415	27%	38%	$4,449	24%
Liquid assets						
Less than $10K	51%	1,501	7%	37%	1,658	4%
$10K-$25K	55%	4,282	28%	41%	3,895	30%
$25K or more	62%	9,160	57%	38%	10,575	58%
Income						
Less than $25K	52%	4,132	24%	32%	3,658	14%
$25K-$50K	62%	4,124	26%	42%	4,587	27%
$50K or more	51%	6,140	38%	48%	5,708	37%
Age						
18-34	51%	2,771	13%	44%	2,210	16%
35-44	54%	3,270	15%	41%	3,347	21%
45-54	50%	3,677	23%	39%	3,310	24%
55-64	55%	4,647	39%	34%	6,296	33%
65+	63%	7,349	48%	32%	9,149	39%

Measuring Market Segment Profitability

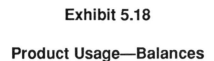

Exhibit 5.18

Product Usage—Balances

	Passbook Savings		Statement Savings	
	% Using	Average Balance	% Using	Average Balance
Total	55%	$4,415	38%	$4,449
Service-assurance Seekers	61%	7,093	40%	5,484
Trendy Credit Buyers	43%	4,464	46%	2,352
Accumulator Leaders	58%	3,404	37%	4,200
Security Driven	61%	3,823	29%	5,028
Traditionalists	57%	3,347	33%	3,210
Institution Dependents	52%	4,537	39%	7,089
Convenience Driven	52%	3,775	31%	4,033
Price Alerts	55%	5,490	38%	4,449

Exhibit 5.17 breaks out passbook and statement usage by various demographics. The passbook and statement accounts are complementary in terms of average balances. However, among age groups, seniors are most likely to have a passbook account and least likely to have a statement account. Balances in both types of accounts increase with age.

High-liquid-asset households are more likely to have a passbook account than a statement account. High-income households are only slightly more likely to have a passbook savings account.

As shown in Exhibit 5.18, Service-assurance Seekers hold the highest-average passbook balances, while Institution dependents are highest in statement balances. Surprisingly, the very rate-sensitive Price Alerts and Accumulator Leaders hold relatively high balances in savings products. This suggests that there is little correlation between rate sensitivity and usage of savings accounts. Trendy Credit Buyers are least likely to have a passbook, and most likely to have a statement account.

97

Product Profitability Measurement Tools

Exhibit 5.19 shows that the MMDA, money market deposit account customer has virtually the same profile as the CD, certificate of deposit customer, although the average MMDA balances tend to be lower. Based on local studies, there are significant cross-sales opportunities within existing customer bases for CD owners who do not have an MMDA with an institution, and for MMDA owners who do not keep a certificate with that institution.

CDs continue to be an important investment for customers over fifty-five years old. Savings institutions dominate over fifty-fives and the thirty-five to forty-four age groups, but commercial banks hold the greatest share of CDs for the eighteen to thirty-four, and the forty-five to fifty-four age.

Exhibit 5.19

Product Usage—Balances

	MMDAs			CDs*		
	% With Product	Average Balance	% 5K+	% With Product	Average Balance	% 5K+
Total	31%	$17,471	51%	32%	$20,408	26%
Liquid assets						
Less than $10K	11%	4,559	10%	14%	4,756	2%
$10K-$25K	38%	8,510	45%	41%	9,660	3%
$25K or more	61%	26,132	69%	57%	33,031	49%
Income						
Less than $25K	23%	14,513	44%	31%	17,749	23%
$25K-$50K	32%	14,616	46%	30%	21,681	25%
$50K or more	53%	24,914	67%	36%	25,327	37%
Age						
18-34	18%	11,852	48%	13%	7,900	9%
35-44	24%	13,673	36%	22%	9,948	11%
45-54	33%	14,792	49%	29%	17,414	28%
55-64	39%	14,620	46%	43%	17,422	24%
65+	43%	26,316	63%	53%	32,068	39%

* The high proportion of CDs under $5,000 resulted from the lowering of account minimums.

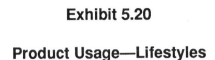

Exhibit 5.20

Product Usage—Lifestyles

	MMDAs		CDs	
	% Using	Average Balance	% Using	Average Balance
Total	31%	$17,471	32%	$20,408
Service-assurance Seekers	36%	18,835	29%	23,700
Trendy Credit Buyers	17%	9,039	15%	6,779
Accumulator Leaders	35%	19,015	31%	26,449
Security Driven	40%	13,862	38%	26,892
Traditionalists	22%	17,148	34%	21,045
Institution Dependents	35%	17,924	46%	14,478
Convenience Driven	20%	7,110	24%	7,992
Price Alerts	47%	23,205	39%	22,791

Exhibit 5.20 shows that MMDAs and CDs also look similar when viewed by lifestyles. Five segments have thirty percent or greater usage of CDs. MMDA account usage is thirty percent greater in five of the eight segments as well.

The Security Driven and the Price Alerts are likely to have both an MMDA and a CD. The CDs of the Security Driven have higher balances, however. Trendy Credit Buyers are least likely to have CD or MMDA accounts. When they do have one of these accounts, the balance is small relative to the other segments. Price Alert households keep more dollars in MMDA accounts than in CDs due to the higher-penetration level. Institution Dependents keep twenty-four percent more in their MMDA accounts compared with their CDs. The Price Alerts are the best MMDA customers in terms of high balances and segment penetration. The Security Driven and Accumulator Leaders have the highest average balance among CD customers.

Relative levels of deposits in MMDA accounts could change as interest rates decline. To the extent that balance levels do not fall, the account may be used to hold funds while the consumer waits for interest rates to rebound.

Exhibit 5.21 shows that the use of IRAs and self-directed IRAs generally increases with assets and income. This finding is not surprising, since these are the people with the capacity to invest. The high balances of self-directed IRAs for high-asset, high-income, and the over fifty-five households probably are influenced significantly by rollovers from company retirement plans.

Exhibit 5.21

Product Usage—Balances

	IRAs			Self-Directed IRAs		
	% With Product	Average Balance	% 5K+	% With Product	Average Balance	% 5K+
Total	33%	$10,379	38%	8%	$16,235	44%
Liquid assets						
Less than $10K	18%	5,976	13%	5%	3,379	10%
$10K-$25K	45%	8,635	34%	14%	13,031	50%
$25K or more	52%	14,761	56%	11%	32,752	71%
Income						
Less than $25K	17%	7,526	27%	3%	8,372	44%
$25K-$50K	41%	8,299	33%	11%	7,744	26%
$50K or more	66%	15,559	53%	21%	29,081	65%
Age						
18-34	22%	6,685	19%	10%	5,668	25%
35-44	36%	8,212	25%	11%	10,480	30%
45-54	42%	10,350	38%	11%	11,768	79%
55-64	47%	14,266	55%	8%	53,480	60%
65+	22%	11,491	46%	2%	24,500	50%

The lifestyle segments who make substantial use of IRAs are reasonably consistent with those same lifestyle groups who maintain substantial investments in CDs and MMDAs. However, average balances in IRAs flatten out substantially when segmented by lifestyle.

Use of self-directed IRAs however is more volatile, with penetration ranging from 3 percent to 15 percent and with balances ranging from just under $5,000 to over $40,000.

Issue: Market Segmentation Profitability

With the foregoing information obtained about customers, it is then possible to project profitability by market segment.

Profitability can be used as a guideline in understanding:

- Current customer franchise, strengths and weaknesses.
- Current institutional strengths and weaknesses.
- Key target market segments for penetration and profit improvement.
- Current gaps that need to be addressed by product development.

Profit Model Description

Exhibit 5.22 is a profit-per-household model for various income groups. The model was constructed using survey data on market share, average balances and the percent of customers in various age and income segments.

Cost data was obtained from the 1985 Federal Reserve (Fed) Functional Cost Analysis Study. When adjustments were made, they were applied consistently, using the following formulas:

- Profit = [(Net Interest Margin x Average Balance) - Expense] x % households having the account

- Income = Average Balance x Earnings Credit (from Fed functional cost analysis)

- Annual Expense = A % from Fed functional costs; or = (Account Acquisition Cost/Estimated Life) + Cost to Receive Payment x 12 mo.

Note: The Fed Functional Cost Analysis Study did not detail as many asset types as were included for the model in Exhibit 5.22. Therefore, the cost figures for several loan types are the same. Although this may make the exact result slightly less accurate for general use, the formula is still valuable. Individual institutions may wish to rebuild this analysis using their own average balances and specific costs.

Example: Savings account profit for forty-five to fifty-four year-old segment.

Information		Sources
Percent with product:	50%	Raddon Research
Average balance:	$3,677	Raddon Research
Annual operating cost:	$49.41	Fed. Functional Cost Analysis Study
Net interest margin:	4.6%	Fed. Functional Cost Analysis Study

Per Household Profitability

Average balance		$	3,677.00
Net interest margin	x		4.6%
Earnings		$	169.14
Less expense	-	$	49.41
Profitability	=	$	119.73
x % holding account	x		50%
Per household profitability		$	*59.87*

Exhibit 5.23 summarizes the profit-per-household data detailed in Exhibit 5.22. The high-income ($50K+) segment is the most profitable group. The overall average profitability of this segment is eight times higher than households earning less than $25,000.

However, households earning less than $25,000, due to their quantity in the population, have almost the same percent of deposit profit as high-income households. If we factored in narrower spreads on deposit dollars because of the sensitivity to rates of high-income households, the deposit profit of low-income households might well exceed that of high-income households taken as a whole.

EXHIBIT 5.22

Profitability By Market Segment - Households By Income

Products		Less Than $25,000		$25,000-$49,000		$50,000 Or More
Total Profit per Household		$329.48		$1,037.77		$2,653.81
Deposit Product Profit		$165.79		$305.63		$745.91
Loan Product Profit		$163.70		$732.15		$1,907.90
Deposit Holdings						
Checking Accounts						
% with Regular/Avg. Balance	50%	$698.40	48%	$912.60	40%	$1,548.00
% with 5 1/4%/Avg. Balance	37%	$2,748.60	43%	$2,970.00	44%	$4,671.00
% with Mrkt. Rate/Avg. Balance	3%	$5,427.00	6%	$10,080.00	14%	$20,295.00
Annual Cost						
Regular Checking		$90.96		$144.96		$140.64
5 1/4%		$118.92		$129.00		$117.00
Market Rate		$123.60		$126.36		$99.00
Interest Margin						
Regular Checking		$61.90		$80.88		$137.20
5 1/4%		$37.99		$123.64		$194.45
Market Rate		$215.07		$399.47		$804.29
Regular Checking Annual Fees		$29.40		$29.40		$29.40
Annual Profitability						
Regular Checking		$0.34		$88.96		$220.41
5 1/4%		($51.53)		$24.04		$106.85
Market Rate		$120.87		$302.51		$734.69
Per HH Profitability		($14.98)		$71.68		$240.46
Savings Accounts						
Percent With Account		51.6%		61.8%		51.0%
Average Balance		$4,132.00		$4,124.00		$6,140.00
Annual Operating Cost		$49.41		$49.41		$49.41
Net Interest Margin		$189.33		$188.96		$281.33
Account Profitability		$139.92		$139.55		$231.92
Per HH Profitability		$72.20		$86.24		$118.28

EXHIBIT 5.22 (Continued)

Products	Less Than $25,000	$25,000-$49,000	$50,000 Or More
MMDA Accounts			
Percent With Account	22.6%	32.2%	53.1%
Average Balance	$14,513.00	$14,616.00	$24,914.00
Annual Operating Cost	$28.88	$28.88	$28.88
Net Interest Margin	$375.02	$377.68	$643.78
Account Profitability	$346.14	$348.80	$614.90
Per HH Profitability	$78.23	$112.31	$326.51
Certificates of Deposit			
Percent with Account	31.2%	29.9%	36.1%
Average Balance	$17,749.00	$21,681.00	$25,327.00
Annual Operating Cost	$27.57	$27.57	$27.57
Net Interest Margin	$131.34	$160.44	$187.42
Account Profitability	$103.77	$132.87	$159.85
Per HH Profitability	$32.38	$39.73	$57.70
IRA Accounts			
Percent With Account	16.9%	41.4%	66.0%
Average Balance	$7,526.00	$8,299.00	$15,559.00
Annual Operating Cost	$27.57	$27.57	$27.57
Net Interest Margin	$15.50	$17.10	$32.05
Account Profitability	($12.07)	($10.48)	$4.48
Per HH Profitability	($2.04)	($4.34)	$2.96
Loan Holdings			
First Mortgages, First Home			
Percent With Loan	23.0%	55.3%	66.7%
Average Balance	$17,349.00	$33,985.00	$56,411.00
Annual Operating Cost	$106.18	$207.99	$345.24
Net Interest Margin	$492.54	$964.83	$1,601.51
Account Profitability	$386.36	$756.85	$1,256.27
Per HH Profitability	$88.86	$418.54	$837.93
First Mortgage On Second Home			
Percent With Loan	1.6%	6.5%	14.3%
Average Balance	$15,529.00	$27,134.00	$49,900.00
Annual Operating Cost	$95.04	$166.06	$305.39
Net Interest Margin	$440.87	$770.33	$1,416.66
Account Profitability	$345.83	$604.27	$1,111.27
Per HH Profitability	$5.53	$39.28	$158.91

EXHIBIT 5.22 (Continued)

Products	Less Than $25,000	$25,000-$49,000	$50,000 Or More
Second Mortgage			
Percent With Account	2.6%	6.8%	6.8%
Average Balance	$19,350.00	$17,000.00	$11,210.00
Annual Operating Cost	$91.88	$91.88	$91.88
Net Interest Margin	$501.16	$440.30	$290.34
Account Profitability	$409.28	$348.42	$198.46
Per HH Profitability	$10.64	$23.69	$13.50
Home Equity Line of Credit			
Percent With Loan	1.4%	5.0%	11.6%
Average Balance	$15,500.00	$19,880.00	$50,064.00
Annual Operating Cost	$98.44	$98.44	$98.44
Net Interest Margin	$401.45	$514.89	$1,296.66
Account Profitability	$303.01	$416.45	$1,198.22
Per HH Profitability	$4.24	$20.82	$138.99
Home Improvement Loan			
Percent With Loan	4.2%	7.1%	4.8%
Average Balance	$4,047.00	$4,100.00	$8,533.00
Annual Operating Cost	$91.88	$91.88	$91.88
Net Interest Margin	$104.82	$106.19	$221.00
Account Profitability	$12.94	$14.31	$129.12
Per HH Profitability	$0.54	$1.02	$6.20
Personal Line of Credit			
Percent With Loan	15.1%	22.2%	35.4%
Average Balance	$474.00	$489.00	$539.00
Annual Operating Cost	$78.76	$78.76	$78.76
Net Interest Margin	$12.28	$12.67	$13.96
Account Profitability	($66.48)	($66.09)	($64.80)
Per HH Profitability	($10.04)	($14.67)	($22.94)
Overdraft Checking			
Percent With Loan	7.9%	16.9%	32.7%
Average Balance	$648.00	$1,053.00	$2,741.00
Annual Operating Cost	$91.88	$91.88	$91.88
Net Interest Margin	$16.78	$27.27	$70.99
Account Profitability	($75.10)	($64.61)	($20.89)
Per HH Profitability	($5.93)	($10.92)	($6.83)

EXHIBIT 5.22 (Continued)

Products	Less Than $25,000	$25,000- $49,000	$50,000 Or More
VISA			
Percent With Loan	36.3%	58.9%	72.1%
Average Balance	$708.00	$1,875.00	$2,305.00
Annual Operating Cost	$71.05	$71.05	$71.05
Net Interest Margin	$124.71	$330.28	$406.03
Account Profitability	$53.66	$259.23	$334.97
Per HH Profitability	$19.48	$152.69	$241.52
MasterCard			
Percent With Loan	26.2%	50.6%	64.6%
Average Balance	$1,287.00	$1,143.00	$2,302.00
Annual Operating Cost	$71.05	$71.05	$71.05
Net Interest Margin	$226.71	$201.34	$405.50
Account Profitability	$155.65	$130.29	$334.44
Per HH Profitability	$40.78	$65.92	$216.05
Travel/Entertainment Card			
Percent With Loan	5.0%	15.7%	34.0%
Average Balance	$1,046.00	$773.00	$3,986.00
Annual Operating Cost	$71.05	$71.05	$71.05
Net Interest Margin	$184.25	$136.16	$702.13
Account Profitability	$113.20	$65.11	$631.08
Per HH Profitability	$5.66	$10.22	$214.57
Auto Loan #1			
Percent With Loan	19.6%	42.3%	38.1%
Average Balance	$4,441.00	$5,464.00	$6,811.00
Annual Operating Cost	$91.88	$91.88	$91.88
Net Interest Margin	$115.02	$141.52	$176.40
Account Profitability	$23.14	$49.64	$84.52
Per HH Profitability	$4.54	$21.00	$32.20
Auto Loan #2			
Percent With Loan	1.4%	6.8%	8.8%
Average Balance	$10,286.00	$5,215.00	$8,428.00
Annual Operating Cost	$91.88	$91.88	$91.88
Net Interest Margin	$266.41	$135.07	$218.29
Account Profitability	$174.53	$43.19	$126.41
Per HH Profitability	$2.44	$2.94	$11.12

EXHIBIT 5.22 (Continued)

Products	Less Than $25,000	$25,000-$49,000	$50,000 Or More
Boat/RV Loan			
Percent With Loan	0.0%	2.7%	6.8%
Average Balance		$6,138.00	$13,056.00
Annual Operating Cost	$91.88	$91.88	$91.88
Net Interest Margin	$0.00	$158.97	$338.15
Account Profitability	($91.88)	$67.09	$246.27
Per HH Profitability	$0.00	$1.81	$16.75
Personal Loan			
Percent With Loan	12.5%	16.0%	21.8%
Average Balance	$2,605.00	$3,503.00	$12,391.00
Annual Operating Cost	$91.88	$91.88	$91.88
Net Interest Margin	$67.47	$90.73	$320.93
Account Profitability	($24.41)	($1.15)	$229.05
Per HH Profitability	($3.05)	($0.18)	$49.93

Exhibit 5.23

Profitability—Income

Income	% of U.S. Households	Household Deposit Profit		Household Loan Profit		Total	
		$	% of Total	$	% of Total	$	% of Total
Less than $25K	53%	$166	31%	$164	15%	$329	20%
$25K-$50K	34%	$306	36%	$732	43%	$1,038	40%
$50K+	13%	$746	33%	$1,907	43%	$2,653	40%

Exhibit 5.24

Profitability—Age

Age	% of U.S. Households	Household Deposit Profit		Household Loans Profit		Total	
		$	% of Total	$	% of Total	$	% of Total
18-34	36%	$85	10%	$874	46%	$959	35%
35-44	23%	157	12%	820	28%	987	23%
45-54	13%	251	12%	687	13%	939	12%
55-64	12%	359	14%	489	9%	848	10%
65+	15%	1,093	53%	242	5%	1,336	20%

Exhibit 5.24 summarizes household profit by the age of consumers. Deposit profit per household increases substantially with age and is highest among the over sixty-five consumer group. That age group, which comprises 15 percent of all households, contributes 53 percent of deposit profitability.

On the other hand, consumers aged eighteen to thirty-four contribute 46 percent of loan profitability. Nine out of ten dollars earned from this group stem from loan products.

Summary

Account profitability is a key pricing consideration in a deregulated rate environment. Factors for consideration include:

- Institution costs and account maintenance
- Account balances
- Interest rate spread between sources and uses of balances
- Account fees

Marketing customer information files (MCIFs) allow an institution to understand multiple relationships held by households and the profitability of the entire relationship. These files allow an institution to view all accounts of a customer household together, just as the customer views the relationship. While the majority of MCIF systems are not tied to the day-to-day operational systems and, therefore do not allow for relationship pricing, technological advances are pointing in this direction. As this develops, financial institutions will be able to identify unprofitable household relationships and charge them service fees accordingly.

The Functional Cost Analysis Program is a venture between the Federal Reserve Banks and participating banks and savings institutions. This program is designed to assist a participating institution in increasing overall earnings, as well as, improving the operational efficiency of each function. Aggregate data is broken down by type of institution (commercial bank versus savings and loan) and by deposit size. This data is helpful in estimating costs when the institution is unable to determine its own costs.

Breakeven analysis involves determining breakeven balances by determining the costs and revenues of each product. Revenue sources are earnings on balances and explicit fees. The net-interest margin—the value to the institution of the depositors' money invested in loans or investments—is the source of all cost recovery and profit to the institution. It is the determining factor of the breakeven balance and is determined by two variables: yield on earning assets and asset mix. The breakeven balance is determined by dividing the annualized deposit operating cost by the net-interest margin minus any reserve requirement.

Marketing efforts should target profitable segments of the consumer base. Consumer research and Fed Functional Cost Analysis data provide the necessary tools to determine market segment profitability. Profitability can be used as a guideline in understanding the current customer franchise, institution strengths and weaknesses, key market segments for penetration and profit improvement, and gaps in the current product line.

Chapter 6

Product Pricing Strategy Execution

Overview of Pricing Strategy Objectives
Guidelines for Pricing Strategy
The Price-Band Concept of Pro-active Pricing
Developing a Pricing Simulation Model
Market Simulation Model
Summary

Chapter 6

Product Pricing Strategy Execution

Overview of Pricing Strategy Objectives

Three fundamental pricing strategies exist to provide support for a financial institution's overall strategic business goals. The appropriateness of each pricing strategy varies at different times, given the dynamic nature of competition in a deregulated environment. It varies at both the overall financial institution level and the specific product level. Pricing strategy reflects the dynamic nature of the product's life cycle and the differing performance objectives associated with each stage of the product's life cycle.

The three pricing strategies are: market-share growth performance, earnings' maximization performance, and targeted growth/financial focus. Whatever management's strategic direction, a pricing strategy reflects degrees of emphasis rather than exclusivity. The reality is that market share and profitability are intertwined within financial performance. Successful product managers consciously shift emphasis among these strategies to maximize their product's financial performance.

Market-Share Growth Performance

A market-share growth performance strategy dictates that the financial institution position itself against the competitive mainstream with its pricing strategy. Market-share growth is accomplished through an emphasis on penetration-pricing tactics. Through such tactics, the financial institution is willing to accept short-term losses in exchange for competitive positioning, which assures long-term market-share growth and profitability. The immediate profitability of a product line or customer relationship is secondary to the benefits anticipated to be derived from long-term market-share growth opportunities. This pricing strategy is most effective when the financial institution anticipates either a critical market-share requirement or an experience-curve-generated cost advantage that must be achieved to sustain its long-term profitability.

Product Pricing Strategy Execution

Within the financial industry, this strategy has been among the most misunderstood ones between savings institutions and commercial banks. Commercial banks typically think savings institutions to be ill-advised with their low-cost checking products. In fact, many savings institutions try to emulate their commercial bank competitors in pricing checking services. The reality is that most savings institutions must attract sufficiently large numbers of checking relationships to support the fixed cost of being in the checking business. Their pricing tactics should be different from the commercial bank's pricing if they wish to profitably sustain a checking product line over the long- term. The key in using penetration-pricing tactics is the financial institution's ability to tolerate short-term losses until the long-term advantages are realized.

Penetration pricing for market-share growth requires that an institution act boldly or not at all. The institution's offer must be sufficiently attractive to overcome the consumer's natural inertia that exists toward change, even change that is in their personal interest. The parameters within which penetration pricing must operate are determined by these factors:

- The amount of profitability the institution is willing to forego
- The period of time it's willing to forego that profitability
- The cost of the offer

The bottom line of this pricing strategy is that the financial institution must be both innovative and proficient at merchandising its financial services. Its associated pricing tactics involve calculated risks that the management of most financial institutions is unwilling to take.

Earnings' Maximization Performance

An earnings' maximization performance strategy dictates that the financial institution take charge of pricing its financial services rather than pricing them in reaction to the competition. The institution's pricing tactics are influenced more by financial self-interests than by the competitive environment in which it operates. It is willing to forego market-share for earnings' maximization opportunities. The institution understands the calculated risks associated with price leadership and is willing to undertake them.

Earnings' maximization is generally achieved through an emphasis upon explicit pricing tactics. The objective of explicit pricing is to move each customer's account, or each financial service delivered, to a profitable status. The revenue stream for each service should be greater than its cost of delivery. Inevitably, explicit pricing becomes the least-competitive pricing tactic. It may not always be the most profitable pricing tactic either, since volume is also an integral component of aggregate product line profitability.

Explicit pricing tactics are effectively used by commercial banks in efforts to underwrite the costs associated with deregulation of the financial industry. Commercial banks use pricing to delineate which portion of their customer base is placed at competitive risk with the introduction of new financial services. This strategy often results in savings institutions having difficult time attracting the commercial banks' most-desirable customer relationships.

The challenge for any institution pursuing an earnings' maximization performance-pricing strategy is to avoid being labeled as non-competitive by its marketplace. The institution must constantly probe the parameters of its marketplace's price-band and become proficient at manipulating product demand to its advantage.

Customer-demand manipulation requires more customer interaction training and sales skills among customer-contact personnel. The institution must leverage all of its assets—convenient locations, quality service, image, etc.—to the maximum. The earnings' maximization strategy requires monitoring competitive rates and the flow of internal funds. Executive management must be more responsive to funds-flow trends and must be willing to constantly fine-tune its interest rate management and pricing practices.

Product pricing is generally done on an explicit basis rather than around bank relationships. The breakeven analysis formula is as follows:

Breakeven Analysis Formula

$$\text{Breakeven Average Balance} = \frac{\text{(Annualized Total Operating Costs - Service Charge Income)}}{\text{(Average Asset Yield)} \times [[1.00 - \text{Float} + \text{Reserves}] - \text{Interest Rate}]}$$

Institutions should attempt to quantify the trade-offs associated with opportunities for reducing interest expenses. The net profit improvement quantification formula is as follows:

Product Pricing Strategy Execution

Net Profit Improvement Quantification Formula

Projected
Net Profit   =   [(A * B) * C] - [(A * D) * E]
Improvement

Where:
A = Average $ Investable Balance Repricing Opportunity
B = Basis Points of Interest Rate Reduction
C = Projected % Deposit Retention
D = Basis Points of Net Interest Margin on Projected Marginal Funds
        Investment Opportunity (i.e. Fed Funds Sold Rate)
E = Projected % Deposit Run-off

In most instances, the duration of the projected net profit improvement parallels that of the "opportunity-interest-margin" lost-dollar value. Whenever either one has a greater duration than the other, adjustments should be made to the formula.

Target Growth/Financial Focus Strategy

Often a financial institution finds it advantageous to pursue a middle-ground strategy between the two extremes of market-share growth and maximization of earnings' performance. By selectively targeting opportunities in both performance areas, the financial institution takes advantage of any opportunities for earnings' maximization to help underwrite market-share growth activities. A portion of the improved earnings' results are used for a bonus rate promotion that will acquire new customers.

The targeted growth/financial focus strategy is management intensive. It requires the careful building of an image that does not send mixed signals to the marketplace about the institution. The strategy concurrently plays both extremes of the marketplace's price-band. The institution's management must constantly walk the tightrope between balanced high-performance results and mediocrity.

A target growth/financial focus strategy requires a significant commitment to product development and the management of product positioning. The financial institution often simultaneously employs different pricing tactics. For example, it may lower the interest rates paid on core consumer deposit products such as MMDAs, SuperNOWs, and CDs, while concurrently launching new rate-sensitive liability products paying introductory bonus interest rates.

The package goods industry has long pursued similar product strategies as a standard part of their market-share growth efforts. Market share growth for any product line typically entails cannibalization from the institution as well as growth from its competition. It is integral to overcoming the price-band hurdle points, whether fee or interest rate related.

Financial services continue to assume more of the characteristics of commodities. During the decade ahead, financial institutions can no longer ignore the importance of becoming high-volume, low-cost providers of financial services. Simply relying on a quality service differentiation alone will not be sufficient to survive in a deregulated environment. The significant financial institution players of the 1990s will have ownership of both positions in the eyes of the financial services user.

Guidelines for Pricing Strategy

Pricing is recognized as one of the most powerful tools of marketing, but is relatively unused as a tool for marketing in the financial industry. Strong earnings performance and market-share growth are often viewed as incompatible by management.

Financial institutions traditionally treated all customers similarly, regardless of their comparative contribution to profit. Today, many financial institutions still rely on their most profitable customers to subsidize the unprofitable ones. Financial industry deregulation has prompted many financial institutions to re-examine both their reluctance to differentiate the level of service provided to various customer segments and their use of pricing incentives.

Employees of financial institutions have often found the art of customer-service differentiation difficult to practice. Executive management and employees alike can expect to find the strategic pricing implications for successfully surviving deregulation even more difficult.

An examination of the patterns of competition within other previously deregulated industries points out the need for two distinct pricing strategies—one for retaining customers and another for acquiring customers.

The focus of the institution's customer-retention strategy should be earnings' maximization. The focus is its customer-acquisition strategy should be potential profitable growth. It is important to understand the role and financial impact of pricing incentives for retaining and acquiring customers. Pricing incentives can be categorized as either "soft-dollar" or "hard-dollar." Soft-dollar pricing incentives don't involve "real" dollar costs for the financial institution. Hard-dollar pricing incentives involve actual costs or revenue losses for the institution.

Several principles exist when using pricing incentives:

- Pricing incentives invariably expand beyond the scope of what is required to attract and/or maintain customer relationships.

- There are diminishing returns in the bundling of pricing incentives to strengthen a customer relationship.

- The continuance of a pricing incentive is seldom a pivotal issue in the customers' decision to retain their financial relationship.

Generally, hard-dollar pricing incentives should be used in the customer relationship acquisition process and then discontinued. Up-front, hard-dollar pricing incentives can facilitate a product's sale if the product has perceived value to the customer. Once the buying decision is made, the long-term continuation of the hard-dollar pricing incentive has little influence on retaining customer relationships if the product lives up to its original perceived value. Customers are more often lost as a result of pricing to recover hard-dollar incentives' cost or revenues than by discontinuing the pricing incentive after a period of time.

Exhibit 6.1 illustrates various pricing incentive-cost or revenue-waiver-recovery requirements in terms of additional investable deposit balances at various product's net-interest margins.

Fee waivers and other hard-dollar pricing incentives should not be permanently built into a customer relationship for the following reasons:

- Long-term product profitability is unnecessarily compromised.

- The product's pricing often exceeds the customer's perceived value of the product.

- Profits derived from existing customer relationships must be used to underwrite the pricing strategy for acquiring new customers.

EXHIBIT 6.1

Account Incentives Average Investable Deposits Requirement* Breakeven Table

* [Average Deposits less (Float + Reserves)]

$ VALUE OF INCENTIVES	1/4	1/2	3/4	1	2	3	4	5	6	7	8	9	10	15
100	40000	20000	13333	10000	5000	3333	2500	2000	1667	1429	1250	1110	100	667
75	30000	15000	10000	7500	3750	2500	1875	1500	1250	1071	937	833	750	500
50	20000	10000	6667	5000	2500	1667	1250	1000	833	714	625	5255	500	333
45	18000	9000	6000	4500	2250	1500	1125	900	750	643	563	500	450	300
40	16000	8000	5333	4000	2000	1333	1000	800	667	571	500	444	400	267
35	14000	7000	4667	3500	1750	1167	875	700	585	500	437	389	350	233
30	12000	6000	4000	3000	1500	1000	750	600	500	429	375	333	300	200
25	10000	5000	333	2500	1250	833	625	500	417	357	312	277	250	167
20	8000	4000	2667	2000	1000	667	500	400	333	285	250	222	200	133
15	6000	3000	2000	1500	750	500	375	300	250	214	188	167	150	100
10	4000	2000	1333	1000	500	333	250	200	167	143	125	111	100	67
9	3600	1800	1200	900	450	300	225	180	150	128	112	100	90	60
8	3200	1600	1067	800	400	267	200	160	133	114	100	89	80	53
7	2800	1400	933	700	350	233	175	140	117	100	88	78	70	47
6	2400	1200	800	600	300	200	150	120	100	86	75	67	60	40
5	2000	1000	667	500	250	167	125	100	84	72	62	55	50	33
4	1600	800	533	400	200	133	100	80	67	57	50	44	40	27
3	1200	600	400	300	150	100	75	60	50	43	37	33	30	20
2	800	400	267	200	100	67	50	40	34	28	24	22	20	14
1	400	200	133	100	50	33	25	20	17	14	12	11	10	7

Net Interest Percent Margin**
(** Average Asset Yield Percent Or Internal Transfer Rate Percent Minus Interest Expense Percent)

Ledger Balance Requirements Conversion Formula:

Average Ledger Balance Requirement = $\dfrac{\text{Average Investable Deposits Required}}{[\text{Collected Balance \% x (1.00 - Reserve \%)}]}$

Premium interest rate offers require careful consideration. Industry experience and the price-band concept lend support to the payment of higher-bonus interest rates for shorter durations as a more effective pricing incentive for acquiring new customers. A compressed bonus-rate period makes it easier to get over the required interest rate differential hurdle that is necessary to overcome the customer's inertia.

The financial impact of a bonus interest rate offer is the function of three management pricing incentive decisions:

- The amount of profitability the institution is willing to forego

- The period of time the institution is willing to forego the profitability

- The period of time the premium rate is to be paid

The formula for calculating bonus interest rates is shown in Exhibit 6.2.

Exhibit 6.2

Premium/Bonus Interest Rate Percent Formula

$$\text{Premium/Bonus Interest Rate \%} = \frac{TP * [\, (ID * IM) - AC\,]}{(ID - PP)}$$

Where:

TP	=	Time of Profitability Willing to Forego
ID	=	Investable Deposits Projected
IM	=	Interest Margin Projected
AC	=	Annual $ Cost
PP	=	Premium/Bonus Period

Special introductory or promotional bonus interest rate offers, temporary fee waivers (e.g., first year), and other hard-dollar expenditures (e.g., free personalized checks) should be limited as pricing incentives for acquiring customers. Such pricing-incentive offers should be of limited duration and designed to encourage customer action on the product that is offered. Provisions should be made for discontinuing the pricing incentive at a future date to ensure the long-term profitability of the customer relationship.

Customer acquisition and retention pricing strategies require a knowledge of the price-band concept. A financial institution must become a pro-active pricer rather than a reactive pricer of financial services if it is to improve earnings' and growth performance. The pro-active pricing of financial services requires an understanding of the price-band concept and knowledge of its parameters within the competitive marketplace.

The Price-Band Concept of Pro-active Pricing

The price-band represents the customer's natural inertia toward changing their current banking relationships. This customer inertia allows financial institutions to improve their earnings' performance. Likewise, prospective customers' inclinations to continue their existing relationships with a financial institution must be overcome by another financial institution if it is to improve its market-share growth performance. By knowing how both the low-end and the high-end parameters of consumer-financial-relationship pricing can change the customers' inertia, financial institutions can use pricing to manipulate the demand for financial services.

The most visible practitioner of demand manipulation is the airline industry. Airlines have adopted a myriad of fares designed to manage their flight-load capacities by manipulating the demand for seating. The more refined practitioners of demand manipulation are the most profitable and market-share dominant airlines since the industry's deregulation.

A price-band for both interest rates and service-charge fees exists in every marketplace. An institution's profits are maximized on their current customer base by determining the point (lower interest rates/ higher service charge fees) at which lost-customer-account profits meet or exceed the additional profits derived from the pricing adjustments on the remaining accounts. Acquiring new customers is maximized by determining the appeal point (higher interest rate/lower service charge fees) required to entice sufficient numbers of additional customers to offset or exceed the diminished profits derived from the current customer base.

The existence of the price-band also requires the recognition that product line simplification, in terms of the number of products offered, is unlikely to satisfy a financial institution's earnings' improvement and market-share growth-performance objectives. A broad product line is required for an institution to fine-tune a product's pricing offers around the price-band. These pricing offers should minimize interest expense and maximize service-charge fee-income for various target markets. A portion of the earnings' improvement realized from current customers is then reinvested by the institution to underwrite financial services offers to acquire new customers. Such offers build market share but have less profit margin.

Exhibit 6.3 provides findings from national consumer research surveys that can be used to illustrate how the price-band concept is utilized to formulate pricing strategy.

Exhibit 6.3

Interest Rate Sensitivity Parameters

Interest Rate Differential Required to Move	Interest Checking	Regular Savings	Money Market Accounts	Certificates of Deposit
.25%	2%	2%	3%	1%
.50%	8%	6%	7%	6%
1.00%	23%	20%	24%	22%
2.00%	42%	39%	46%	43%
4.00% or more	58%	59%	63%	64%
Won't move	19%	17%	17%	17%

Utilizing these national research findings, financial institutions could formulate either a customer profitability or a customer acquisition pricing strategy. If the strategic objective is to maximize the acquisition of customers, the institution might offer an interest rate premium of 200 or more basis points above competitors to entice a sufficiently large percentage of the market to switch financial institutions. If the strategic objective is to maximize customer profitability, the institution might elect to pay 50 to 100 basis points lower for customer deposits than its marketplace competitors without sustaining an unacceptable level of customer deposit disintermediation.

The principal of the interest rate price-band was perhaps most-graphically illustrated during the introduction of the money market deposit account. The market-share growth winners during the introductory phase were the financial institutions that offered extremely high, albeit short-term, bonus interest rates to attract new depositors. Institutions that elected to offer a lower interest-rate premium for a sustained period of time were generally less successful in attracting new depositors from their competitors. This phenomenon underscores the importance of an institution meeting or exceeding the price-band's upper parameter interest rate hurdle by attracting sufficiently large numbers of new depositor relationships to warrant the additional interest expense. The fact that a high percentage of these new customers were retained by institutions after their interest rates were lowered—if the rates paid stayed within the marketplace's lower parameter "interest rate threshold"—illustrates the flip-side of the price-band concept.

There is a myriad of different pricing tactics that provide the strategic framework for acquiring customers and/or maximizing customer profitability. Interest rate pricing tactics include a variety of alternatives, each of which can influence a specific product's appeal to consumers and its customer relationship profitability.

Deposit Balance Payment Basis

The cornerstone of interest rate pricing tactics is the deposit balance payment basis upon which interest is paid. Interest rates can be paid on any one of three types of deposit balances:

- Ledger balances—the traditional book balance
- Collected balances—the ledger balance minus float
- Investable balances—the ledger balance minus float and any required legal reserves

Product Pricing Strategy Execution

Financial institutions have traditionally paid interest on the basis of ledger deposit balances for consumer interest-bearing deposit accounts. The rationale for this approach was that the consumer would not be able to understand any other basis for interest payment.

The advent of money market accounts paying double digit interest rates prompted many financial institutions to break with tradition and pay interest on a collected-balance basis. While this transition was embraced with much trepidation at the time, it subsequently proved to be another pricing nonevent.

Low-interest rate environments, barring regulatory prohibition, may provide yet another opportunity to better manage interest expenses. Such environments present a unique opportunity to complete the migration from an interest-rate payment basis all the way to investable balances. When interest rates are low, the impact of this change is more transparent because of the minor changes in the amount of interest earned on an individual customer basis. This pricing tactic could provide an impressive earnings' improvement opportunity for many financial institutions, even in a low-interest rate environment. The impact on bottom-line financial performance is of even greater value whenever interest rates are in a rising rate cycle.

Length of Terms for Compounding Interest

The selection of the length of a term for compounding interest is a significant pricing decision. National research has confirmed the consumer's awareness of and preference for greater compounding frequency. The compounding terms offered by the financial institution significantly affect its cost of funds and consequently its net-interest margin. Exhibit 6.4 illustrates the cost of funds impact of this decision.

Deregulation has begun to make obsolete the use of interest rate compounding as an effective competitive tool. Financial institutions' past reliance on compounding was driven by their need to circumvent regulatory interest rate ceilings and to gain a competitive edge. In high-interest rate environments, it is unlikely that financial institutions will receive sufficient competitive benefit from aggressive compounding to offset the significant cost-of-funds increases shown in Exhibit 6.4—Compounding Yield Comparisons.

Exhibit 6.4

Compounding Yield Comparisons

Simple	Daily	Monthly	Quarterly	Semiannual
5.00%	5.13%	5.12%	5.09%	5.06%
6.00%	6.18%	6.17%	6.14%	6.09%
7.00%	7.25%	7.23%	7.19%	7.12%
8.00%	8.33%	8.30%	8.24%	8.16%
9.00%	9.42%	9.35%	9.31%	9.20%
10.00%	10.52%	10.47%	10.38%	10.25%
11.00%	11.63%	11.57%	11.46%	11.30%
12.00%	12.75%	12.68%	12.55%	12.36%
13.00%	13.88%	13.80%	13.65%	13.42%
14.00%	15.02%	14.93%	14.75%	14.49%
15.00%	16.18%	16.08%	15.87%	15.56%

Interest Rate Indexing

Interest rate indexing has both financial and competitive performance implications. The advantage of indexing is its provision of a constant comparative yardstick for the customer to evaluate the relative merits of investment alternatives and to release the customer from the burden of managing and monitoring investment decisions.

The disadvantage of indexing is the sacrifice of management's prerogative to establish interest rates in response to their financial institution's unique asset/liability requirements, earnings' performance needs, and/ or competitive marketplace pressures. Any one or more of these influences might dictate a management decision either to lead or to lag behind the market in its interest rate adjustments.

Most financial institutions find that their financial and competitive performance interests are better served by the flexibility offered by an administered rate index set at the discretion of management and continually monitored, rather than by a published rate index over which they have no control.

Similarly, the use of guaranteed interest rate floors within product designs is being re-evaluated. The volatility and breadth of parameter of interest rate cycles in a deregulated environment make interest rate floors a less-effective pricing tactic from both a competitive and an interest-expense management perspective. In addition, it confuses the competitive positioning between fixed- and variable-interest rate products.

Interest Rate Penalties

Early withdrawal interest rate penalties are yet another pricing tactic issue. It is obviously less an issue in a falling interest rate environment than in a rapidly rising one. Most financial institutions are finding that traditional, minimum early withdrawal penalties provide little protection against disintermediation during an escalating interest rate cycle. As customers become better informed about financial investment alternatives and more astute managers of their assets, minimum early withdrawal penalties will become an even less effective deterrent.

Low-interest rate cycles provide an opportune time to incorporate a disintermediation safety valve in the design of interest-rate-sensitive liability products. The incorporation of a mark-to-market replacement penalty feature within the early withdrawal penalty provides additional protection against disintermediation during periods of rapidly escalating interest rates. The replacement penalty reduces the incentive to switch to other investment alternatives for higher interest rates.

The mark-to-market replacement penalty feature can be calculated several ways. It is most equitably applied, from the customer's perspective, when the replacement interest rate that is used in the mark-to-market replacement interest-expense calculation is based upon a period of time equivalent to the early withdrawal period. Under this concept, the replacement interest rate that is utilized in the penalty calculation is the interest rate paid for a certificate of deposit of the same maturity as the early withdrawal time period. Typically, the early withdrawal penalty becomes the greater of the minimum penalty established for the term of the deposit instrument or the mark-to-market penalty calculation. The financial institution is protected by providing a means of compensation for replacement funds in the form of the early withdrawal penalty. Exhibit 6.5 illustrates the mark-to-market calculation process.

Exhibit 6.5

Mark-to-Market Replacement Penalty

The replacement interest cost differential early withdrawal penalty is calculated as follows:

1. Calculate the amount of interest which would be earned on the CD between the date of withdrawal and the original date of maturity at its original contract interest rate.

2. Calculate the amount of interest which would be earned on the CD between the date of withdrawal and the original date of maturity at the current interest rate for a CD which has a maturity equivalent to the days remaining in the original term of the CD being prematurely withdrawn.

3. Subtract the calculation from step 1 from the calculation in step 2 to determine the amount of the replacement interest cost differential early withdrawal penalty.

The actual early withdrawal penalty incurred is *the greater* of the minimum penalty amount for the time deposit's original contract maturity *or* the amount of the replacement interest cost differential penalty as calculated in step 2 above.

Product Pricing Strategy Execution

Interest Rate Tiers

The use of interest rate tiers as a pricing tactic is widespread throughout the financial industry, in particular, within the savings industry segment. The rationale for utilizing interest rate tiers centers upon these objectives:

- To encourage the consolidation of funds by using interest rate inducements

- To achieve a target cost-of-funds standard for all deposit ranges

- To create the perception of a more competitive interest rate within the marketplace

- To be selectively competitive at certain deposit balance levels

An interest rate tier structure can be used either aggressively or passively to position a liability product. Tiering is a useful tool for changing the perceived competitiveness of a financial product without adversely affecting the net-interest expense target for a specific pool of deposits. Exhibit 6.6 provides the formula for arriving at the weighted cost of funds for a specific pool of deposits.

Exhibit 6.6

Interest Rate Tiers Weighted Cost-of-Funds Formula

$$WFC = [A * (MR - X)] + (B * MR) + [C * (MR + Y)]$$

Where:

WFC	=	Weighted Cost of Funds
MR	=	Market Rate Paid on Funds
A, B, & C	=	% of Dollar Deposits within Tier
X & Y	=	Basis Point Differential from Market Interest Rate for Each Deposit Tier

Tiering interest rates is only an effective pricing tactic when the deposit balances of a product are broadly distributed. Many financial institutions find that after a product's deposit balances have been stratified, a high percentage of them will qualify for the highest-interest rate tier. Under such circumstances, tiering is of little strategic financial value, and other pricing tactics should be employed by the financial institution.

In addition to establishing the interest rate differentials for product tiers, there are two other important decisions that must be made. First, the deposit-balance thresholds must be established for both the interest rate differentials and, if applicable, any service charges. The lower the deposit-balance threshold is, relative to the interest rate percentage differentials or service charge assessment structure, the greater a product's market appeal will be. The higher the deposit-balance thresholds are, the more limited is the product's market appeal.

The second decision is the number of tiers to be offered. The most important guideline is not to lose sight of the original objective for the tiered product offering. Simple tier structures are more easily understood and communicated by the financial institution's sales staff. They are also more easily subjected to competitive comparisons by customers. More complex tier structures enable the financial institution to fine-tune its pricing to be more reflective of its objectives for acquiring customers and/or improving financial performance.

Experience has shown that the tier structure for any given product should not exceed four levels and should preferably be limited to only three levels. If an institution's financial and/or competitive objectives dictate the need for more than four different tiers, the institution should instead offer additional products.

Geographic Interest Rate Sensitivity Factor

Interest rates vary significantly across the country. More financial institutions are evaluating competitive tactics designed to attract funds from outside their traditional geographical markets. Other institutions are considering tactics to combat the entry of a host of new competitors for their traditional customer base franchise.

The relaxation and breakdown of traditional protective regulatory constraints on competition have shaken the "competitive-islands" operating mentality of many institutions. Important segments of the customer base are more financially sophisticated and now are more accessible through advances in direct-marketing capabilities.

Although national research findings suggest that any redefinition of the competitive marketplace will be an evolutionary process, this should not be discounted as a future trend for competition. Location and convenience continue to be dominant criteria for placement of funds. The industry's financial problems are adding another criteria to the customer's decision process about placement of funds—an institution's strength and stability, particularly in the economically depressed sectors of the country are becoming more important.

During the 1990s, many institutions will experience formidable outside competition for their upscale customers whenever convenience is not a legitimate product issue. Credit cards and money market investment products will be the most frequently extended competitive battlegrounds. Exhibit 6.7 points out the diminishing sensitivity to interest rates that exists with geographic distance.

The research findings about the interest rate differentials needed to attract funds from outside a financial institution's geographic marketplace reinforces the notion of prioritizing cross-selling to the institution's existing customers. The findings further underscore the concept of the interest rate price-band hurdle, as well as the difficulties to be encountered when attempting to steal market share from the competition.

Since 90 percent of the financial institutions within any given marketplace price within 100 basis points of each other, it will be difficult to achieve significant market share growth utilizing an institution's traditional product-line services. Future market share growth will more likely come with the introduction of new rate-sensitivity liability products that pay substantial bonus, or premium introductory interest rates.

Developing a Pricing Simulation Model

Utilizing consumer research and internal cost data, financial institutions can develop a pricing model that enables them to price products in a manner that will achieve organizational goals for earnings and market share. The following example of pricing checking accounts utilizes a national consumer survey of 1,022 households conducted in the spring of 1987 for the FIMA/Raddon Strategic Research & Planning Program.

Pricing Checking Accounts

A checking account pricing strategy should be determined by an institution's current strategic customer franchise and strategic objectives.

Exhibit 6.7

Geographic Interest Rate Sensitivity

Percentage Required For Switch	Local Institution Already Using	Local Institution Not Using	Institution in Nearby Community	An Out-of-State Institution
.25%	0.8%	0.6%	0.4%	0.4%
.50%	6%	4%	2%	0.6%
.75%	7%	5%	3%	0.6%
1.00%	20%	15%	9%	3%
2.00%	41%	33%	22%	9%
3.00%	52%	45%	33%	15%
Won't Move	12%	15%	30%	53%

The two main pricing strategies focus on earnings' improvement and market-share growth. To work effectively with either strategy, individually or collectively for checking, it is essential to gain insights into consumers' pricing sensitivity regarding the components of checking accounts.

To price checking accounts, it is necessary to know the value that consumers place on each component of checking account pricing, and the relation that each pricing component has to the others. To gain this understanding, a research technique known as conjoint analysis can be used.

Conjoint analysis, which has also been called "trade-off" analysis, makes it possible to break down a product into its components and to measure how the consumers' value each specific component. With the information on consumers values, the market's reaction to a product or service can be simulated. The simulation of the market's reaction to a product gives a "preference share" for a product in terms of its market appeal. Using this preference share for a product, and the profit margin on each alternative, an institution can make optimal decisions for pricing based on earnings, market share, and competitive analysis. This information allows an institution either to change pricing of existing ac-

Product Pricing Strategy Execution

EXHIBIT 6.8

Checking Utilities

| | Type of Checking Account Currently Held | | | |
Minimum Balance	All Consumers	Non-Interest	Interest	Market Rate
None	73.9	79.2	74.0	53.6
$100	64.1	68.9	63.9	45.8
$300	44.5	48.5	43.6	30.1
$500	26.4	28.6	25.9	15.5
$1,000	14.1	14.65	13.4	8.7
$1,500	1.8	.7	1.0	1.8
Interest Rate				
Market	58.49	49.7	65.3	85.8
5-1/4%	44.28	37.9	49.2	54.9
4%	33.76	29.0	37.5	41.8
3%	25.32	21.9	28.23	31.38
0%	.88	.6	.3	.0
Monthly Fee				
$0	54.45	54.1	58.3	52.1
$3	24.61	22.1	26.7	20.2
$5	1.28	0.3	0.4	0.0
Per Check Charge				
$0	59.13	60.5	60.2	61.3
$.10	24.11	21.6	25.6	23.8
$.20	1.46	0.8	0.7	0.5

counts to maximize earnings and minimize adverse consumer reaction, or to price a product for profitable market share growth.

In this example, consumers were asked to rate the attractiveness of several checking accounts. The accounts varied by interest rate, minimum balance requirement, monthly fees, and charge per check.

Exhibit 6.8 shows the utilities, or values, consumers placed on these checking account features. Utilities are a relative measure of the value that consumers place on the individual product's attributes at a given price level. When utilities are added together, the relative attractiveness of different products can be compared as shown in Exhibit 6.9.

Exhibit 6.9

Product Comparison

	Account 1		Account 2	
	Feature	Utilities	Feature	Utilities
Rate	5-1/4%	44.20	4%	37.76
Minimum balance	$1,000	14.10	$500	26.40
Monthly fee	$5	1.28	$3	24.60
Per check fee	$.10	24.11	$.20	1.46
Total value		83.69		90.22

Exhibit 6.10 isolates interest rate and minimum balance so as to understand their interrelationship. For the total market, accounts with market rates and a $500 minimum have roughly the same utility as accounts with 5-1/4% interest rates and $300 minimum balances. Though not shown in the table, a $200 minimum-balance, 4 percent interest rate checking account would have the same appeal.

> *Example:* If the goal is to attract market-rate checking account holders from competitors non-interest-bearing checking base,

Product Pricing Strategy Execution

EXHIBIT 6.10

Rate Versus Minimum Comparison - Product Utilities

All Households

Minimum		Rate		
	Market	5-1/4%	4%	0%
$0	133.39	118.18	107.66	74.78
$100	123.59	108.38	97.86	64.98
$300	103.99	88.78	78.26	45.38
$500	85.89	70.68	60.16	27.28
$1,000	73.59	58.38	47.86	14.98
$1,500	61.29	46.08	35.56	2.68

Regular Checking Holders

Minimum		Rate		
	Market	5-1/4%	4%	0%
$0	128.90	117.10	108.20	79.80
$100	118.67	106.87	97.97	69.57
$300	98.20	86.40	77.50	49.10
$500	78.30	66.50	57.60	29.20
$1,000	64.35	52.55	43.65	15.25
$1,500	50.40	38.60	29.70	1.30

compare the far left column with the far right column of Exhibit 6.10 in the regular checking holders table. A $1,000 market-rate checking product will have higher value to any non-interest bearing account holder whose minimum balance requirement is over $100, provided other account features are equal.

Exhibit 6.11 compares interest rates and minimum balance requirements for market rate and interest-bearing checking account holders. Current holders of interest-bearing checking accounts place almost equal value on a $1,500 minimum-balance, market-rate product as on a $100-minimum, noninterest-bearing account.

Exhibit 6.11

Product Utilities:
Comparison of Rate versus Minimum Balance

Interest Checking Account Holders

Minimum Balance	Market	5-1/4%	4%	0%
		Rate		
$0	139.30	123.20	111.54	74.30
$100	129.20	113.10	101.44	64.20
$300	108.90	92.80	81.14	43.90
$500	91.20	75.10	63.44	26.20
$1,000	78.75	62.65	50.99	13.75
$1,500	66.30	50.20	38.54	1.30

Market Rate Checking Account Holders

Minimum Balance	Market	5-1/4%	4%	0%
		Rate		
$0	139.40	108.50	95.44	53.50
$100	131.57	100.67	87.61	45.77
$300	115.90	85.00	71.94	30.10
$500	101.30	70.40	57.34	15.50
$1,000	94.45	63.55	50.49	8.65
$1,500	87.60	56.70	43.64	1.80

The high value that market rate checking holders place on rate makes it impossible to price a noninterest account as attractively as any market rate/minimum balance combination. For example, if all other features are equal, a $1,500 market rate checking account's utility of 87.6 is 63 percent higher than the $0 minimum, 0% checking utility of 53.5.

Exhibit 6.12 isolates rate/minimum balance trade-offs for individuals based on the current minimum balance that they maintain in the main household checking account. The values associated with noninterest-bearing checking accounts do not vary among the three groups. However, checking account holders with higher balances place greater importance on interest rate and are more willing to maintain a minimum to earn the interest rate than are account holders in the other groups.

Market Simulation Model

One of the more powerful uses of conjoint analysis is the ability to simulate consumer reaction and profitability for different checking products. Consumer preference share shows the total utility of a product, and allows an institution to estimate its attractiveness.

A product's appeal and profitability are juxtaposed in conjoint analysis. According to Exhibits 6.8—6.12, the ideal product for the consumer is a no-minimum, market-rate checking account. The most profitable account to a financial institution is a $1,500 minimum, noninterest-bearing checking account with a $5 flat fee (see Exhibit 6.13) and a $.20-per-check charge when balances drop below the minimum.

A market simulation model enables an institution to price for profitable earnings' maximization, market-share growth, or a blended strategy.

Exhibit 6.13 shows that the annual earnings for checking accounts *per account* range from a profit of $315 to a loss of $13. In general, the more profitable an account is, the lower its product preference share is. Product preference share ranges from 3.96 to 97.20.

If an institution's pricing strategy is to maximize earnings on a product basis, a high per-unit profit account that has a reasonable level of market acceptance should be selected. The $1,500-minimum-balance, 5.25 percent checking account, with a $3 monthly fee, has a profit of $75 per year and a preference share of 70.69.

EXHIBIT 6.12

Rate/Minimum Trade-Offs - By Current Minimum Balance Maintained

Maintain Balance Less Than $500

Minimum	Market	5-1/4%	4%	0%
			Rate	
$0	134.70	120.00	110.49	81.40
$100	123.20	108.50	98.99	69.90
$300	100.20	85.50	75.99	46.90
$500	80.50	65.80	56.29	27.20
$1,000	66.85	52.15	42.64	13.55
$1,500	54.60	39.90	30.39	1.30

Maintain Balance $500 to $1,000

Minimum	Market	5-1/4%	4%	0%
			Rate	
$0	136.50	123.80	112.85	78.10
$100	127.03	114.33	103.39	68.63
$300	108.10	95.40	84.45	49.70
$500	85.40	72.70	61.75	27.00
$1,000	71.65	58.95	48.00	13.25
$1,500	59.70	47.00	36.05	1.30

Maintain Balance $1,000 plus

Minimum	Market	5-1/4%	4%	0%
			Rate	
$0	128.50	130.30	118.16	77.70
$100	120.57	120.83	108.69	68.23
$300	104.70	101.90	89.76	49.30
$500	89.90	79.20	67.06	26.60
$1,000	79.90	83.40	71.26	12.85
$1,500	72.70	53.50	41.36	.90

EXHIBIT 6.13

Checking Per Account Earnings Maximization

Minimum	Rate	Monthly Fee	Product Preference	x	Annual Profit	=	Profit Index
$1,500	0%	$5	3.96		$315		1,247
$1,500	0%	$3	27.29		$311		8,487
$1,000	0%	$5	16.26		$180		2,927
$1,000	0%	$3	39.59		$176		6,968
$1,500	4%	$5	36.84		$135		4,973
$1,500	4%	$3	60.17		$131		7,882
$750	0%	$5	21.90		$113		2,464
$750	0%	$3	45.23		$109		4,907
$1,500	5.25%	$5	47.36		$79		3,730
$1,500	5.25%	$3	70.69		$75		5,284
$1,000	4.%	$5	49.14		$60		2,948
$1,000	4.%	$3	72.47		$56		4,058
$1,500	6%	$5	61.57		$45		2,771
$500	0%	$5	28.56		$45		1,285
$1,500	6%	$3	84.90		$41		3,481
$500	0%	$3	51.89		$41		2,127
$1,000	5.25%	$5	59.66		$23		1,342
$750	4%	$5	54.78		$22		1,233
$1,000	5.25%	$3	82.99		$19		1,535
$750	4%	$3	78.11		$18		1,445
$400	0%	$5	37.56		$18		676
$400	0%	$3	60.89		$14		852
$1,000	6%	$5	73.87		$0		0
$1,000	6%	$3	97.20		($4)		-389
$750	5.25%	$5	65.30		($6)		-367
$300	0%	$5	46.70		($9)		-420
$750	5.25%	$3	88.63		($10)		-853
$300	0%	$3	70.03		($13)		-910

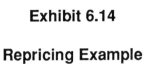

Exhibit 6.14

Repricing Example

	Current Account	Alternatives		
		1	2	3
Rate	0%	0%	0%	0%
Minimum balance	$400	$400	$500	$500
Fee for below balance	$3	$5	$3	$5
Utility	60.89	37.56	51.89	28.56
Percent change		(38%)	(15%)	(53%)
Profit	$14	$18	$41	$45
Percent change		28%	192%	220%

Exhibit 6.14 is an example of how a market simulation model can be used to reprice existing accounts. The table shows the relative change in profit and customer utility that result from repricing. It should be noted that other variables in local markets will affect the outcome of repricing. The profit impact should be based on current account distribution, utilities held by account holders, and competitive prices.

The optimal repricing in this example is a move to a $500 minimum balance with no change in monthly fee. Customer utility will only decline by 15 percent and profit will increase 192 percent.

If the objective is market-share maximization, Exhibit 6.15 illustrates that the more popular products should have no minimums or fees, and should pay interest. The profitability assumption puts the average balances in these accounts at $300. If that is the actual case, then a loss occurs on each account that is acquired.

EXHIBIT 6.15

Market Share Growth

Minimum	Rate	Monthly Fee	Product Preference	Annual Profit	Profit Index
$0	6%	$0	186.85	($91)	-17,003
$0	5.25%	$0	172.64	($89)	-15,322
$0	4%	$0	162.12	($85)	-13,780
$100	6%	$3	147.22	($85)	-12,514
$200	6%	$3	137.43	($76)	-10,445
$100	5.25%	$3	133.01	($83)	-11,007
$0	0%	$0	129.24	($73)	-9,435
$300	6%	$3	127.64	($67)	-8,552
$100	6%	$5	123.89	($81)	-10,035
$200	5.25%	$3	123.22	($72)	-8,810
$100	4%	$3	122.49	($79)	-9,677
$400	6%	$3	118.50	($58)	-6,873
$200	6%	$5	114.10	($72)	-8,215
$300	5.25%	$3	113.43	($60)	-6,834
$200	4%	$3	112.70	($64)	-7,213
$100	5.25%	$5	109.68	($79)	-8,637
$500	6%	$3	109.50	($49)	-5,366
$300	6%	$5	104.31	($63)	-6,572
$400	5.25%	$3	104.29	($49)	-5,110
$300	4.00%	$3	102.91	($49)	-5,043
$750	6%	$3	102.84	($27)	-2,725
$200	5.25%	$5	99.89	($68)	-6,743
$100	4.00%	$5	99.16	($75)	-7,437
$1,000	6%	$3	97.20	($ 4)	-389
$500	5.25%	$3	95.29	($38)	-3,597
$400	6%	$5	95.17	($54)	-5,139
$400	4%	$3	93.77	($34)	-3,188
$300	5.25%	$5	90.10	($56)	-5,068
$100	0%	$3	89.61	($67)	-6,004
$200	4%	$5	89.37	($60)	-5,362
$750	5.25%	$3	88.63	($10)	-853
$500	6%	$5	86.17	($45)	-3,878
$1,500	6%	$3	84.90	$41	3,481
$500	4%	$3	84.77	($19)	-1,611
$1,000	5.25%	$3	82.99	$19	1,535

Exhibit 6.16

Checking Market Share/Profit Maximization

Minimum Balance	Rate	Monthly Fee	Product Preference	Annual Profit	Profit Index
$1,500	0%	$3	27.29	$311	8,487
1,500	4%	$3	60.17	131	7,882
1,000	0%	$3	39.59	176	6,968
1,500	5.25%	$3	70.69	75	5,284
1,500	4%	$5	36.84	135	4,973
750	0%	$3	45.23	109	4,907
1,000	4%	$3	72.47	56	4,058
1,500	5.25%	$5	47.36	79	3,730
1,500	6%	$3	84.90	41	3,481
1,000	4%	$5	49.14	60	2,948
1,000	0%	$5	16.26	180	2,927
1,500	6%	$5	61.57	45	2,771
750	0%	$5	21.90	113	2,464
500	0%	$3	51.89	41	2,127
1,000	5.25%	$3	82.99	19	1,535
750	4%	$3	78.11	18	1,445
1,000	5.25%	$5	59.66	23	1,342
500	0%	$5	28.56	45	1,285
1,500	0%	$5	3.96	315	1,247
750	4%	$5	54.78	22	1,233
400	0%	$3	60.89	14	852
400	0%	$5	37.56	18	676
1,000	6%	$5	73.87	0	0
750	5.25%	$5	65.30	(6)	-367
1,000	6%	$3	97.20	(4)	-389
300	0%	$5	46.70	(9)	-420
750	5.25%	$3	88.63	(10)	-853

Product Pricing Strategy Execution

Assumptions:

> Average balance: 3 times the minimum required
>
> Earning asset yield: 9%
>
> Annual cost per account: $100
>
> Fee: Assessed twice per year, or on 16% of accounts in a given month
>
> Profit Index: Preference Share x Annual Profit
>
> Market Rate: 6%

Industry experience has shown that average balances in no-minimum accounts range from $400 to $600. Nonsufficient funds' charges make a substantial contribution to the profitability of these accounts.

The highest-valued product that shows a profit is a $1,500-minimum, market-rate checking account, with a $3 fee when balances drop below the minimum.

Exhibit 6.16 examines a blend of market attractiveness and profit. A strategy of profitable market-share growth combines profit-per-account with consumer preferences. Profit value tends to affect the profit index more substantially than does preference value in this model. The product line should select profitable products with a preference of at least fifty or greater. The higher-profit numbers tend to outweigh the product utility numbers, thus slightly biasing the model toward profit.

Summary

Financial institutions support their overall strategic business goals utilizing market-share growth performance, earnings' maximization performance, or targeted growth/financial-focus pricing strategies. Organizations do not use one pricing strategy exclusively, marketing efforts are a blend of these three strategies. Periodically, an institution will alter the pricing blend to achieve stated goals and objectives. An example of this would be a short-term rate promotion that acquires new business, followed by a lowering of rates to bring down the cost of funds.

Rarely is one pricing strategy appropriate for all competitive situations or throughout a product's life cycle.

Market-share, growth-performance pricing strategies require the institution to position itself against the competitive mainstream even at the sacrifice of short-term profits. These strategies are effectively applied whenever there exists a critical market-share requirement or experience curve generated cost advantage that is integral to sustain the long-term profitability of a product.

Earnings' maximization pricing strategies dictate taking a pro-active pricing leadership position in the competitive marketplace. These strategies are most effectively applied whenever an established market-share position which can be selectively protected, or financial self-interest considerations exist that warrant the undertaking of calculated risks of market share loss risks.

Targeted growth/financial-focus pricing strategies selectively target opportunities in both market share growth and financial performance areas. These strategies are most effectively applied whenever sufficient financial, time, and management resources exist to support the ownership of both high volume/low cost provider and perceived value differentiation positions in the eyes of the marketplace.

Concurrent strong earnings and market-share growth performance require distinctive pricing strategies for acquiring and retaining customers. Pricing incentives are most cost-effective when used to support the acquisition of customers. Long-term use of pricing incentives for retaining customers often impairs the profitability of accounts, or results in cost-recovery pricing that exceeds the account's perceived value.

Profitable institutions in a deregulated environment manipulate customer demand through pro-active pricing. Pro-active pricers who understand their marketplace's price-band parameters for fees and interest rates are to maximize both profits and the acquisition of customers. Financial institutions utilize a variety of interest rate pricing tactics to provide a strategic framework to maximize the acquisition of customer and/or profitability. These pricing tactics include deposit-balance payment basis, varied compounding terms, rate indexing, early withdrawl penalties, and rate tiers.

Having a firm understanding of product profitability and consumer pricing preferences enables a firm to price their product line to achieve the chosen strategic objectives. A pricing simulation model that blends conjoint analysis with a product's data allows for sound pricing decisions.

Chapter 7

Product Communication Strategy

Elements of a Communication Plan
Budget Preparation
Internal/External Implementation of a Communication Plan
Summary
Sample Communication Pieces

Chapter 7

Product Communication Strategy

The foundation for a marketing communication plan is based on market segmentation research, as previously discussed in Chapter 3. Just as product design is guided by the needs of the market as determined through careful analysis of various sources of research information, likewise the marketing message should be created from the same fact-based process. The advertising strategy and the creative strategy should be developed based on the same analysis of customer's needs and wants that drove the product design.

Further, the media plan should be driven by market-segment analysis. The habits and characteristics of market segments should determine the media that is used to deliver the marketing message. While the logic of this is obvious, it all too often is not the case in reality. Somewhere in the communication-planning process a breakdown often occurs and a less effective campaign results. The reasons for the breakdown range from budget constraints to a lack of creative execution, media planning, or employee training.

On the other hand, a serious communication-planning effort generally results in an effective new product introduction campaign. The first step in communication planning is to realize that few situations will exist when both optimum time and budget will permit the planning and execution of the ideal campaign. The challenge, therefore, becomes to maximize the time and resources *available* by planning creatively. This means understanding all the elements that an optimum plan *could* include and prioritizing them based on what is most effective for the current situation.

Elements of a Communication Plan

A typical communication plan is illustrated in Exhibit 7.1. The first item in each phase of the plan is *objectives*. In reality, however, objectives are

Product Communication Strategy

EXHIBIT 7.1

Communications Plan Flow Chart

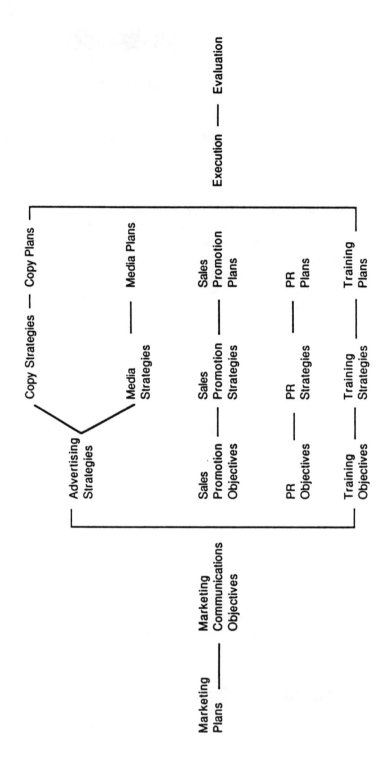

often the most-overlooked—but the most-critical—element of any plan. Without specific guidance in terms of tasks to be accomplished, an effective communication plan is largely an accident. However, in many cases the jump is made directly from product description to creating advertising concepts without sufficient attention to exactly what the proposition is that advertising should deliver to prospective customers within the targeted market.

Advertising strategies depend on the reading and viewing habits of various market segments. For example, the upscale market segments have a tendency to read more and to watch television less than other market segments.

The integration of separate elements of the communication mix—advertising, sales promotion, public relations, and training—becomes the timetable for executing the plan. It may seem obvious, but is worth mentioning, that internal communications and training should be planned well in advance of the other elements. In that way, employees are aware of an ad or promotion before they see it in the paper, or, worse yet, learn about it from a customer.

Budget Preparation

Financial results ultimately determine the success of any marketing program or new product. Maximizing profits depends on spending enough to get the job done without spending more than is necessary. There is a measure of truth in the old story about the advertising manager who said, "I know I'm wasting half of my advertising dollars. The trouble is, I can't figure out which half." At best, gross rating points and ad frequency are effective guidelines. Direct mail is more easily measured, but when a 1 percent to 5 percent response is considered highly successful, the list selection process is obviously inefficient.

There are three budget-setting methods that can be used to determine an appropriate level of spending and to minimize wasted effort. The three methods are:

- Historical method

- Per-unit or percentage-of-sales method

- Task method

149

Product Communication Strategy

Historical Method

As the name suggests, the historical method of budget development is based on previous spending levels. The most often used application of the procedure is for establishing the budget, or actual dollars, spent in a similar situation in the past. Add to that dollar number a factor for inflation and that becomes the total budget. This can be an excellent budget guideline in two situations:

1. A situation in which a program of similar scope has recently been executed and has generated quantifiable positive results. In such a case, it is critical that the objectives are similar and the audience is smaller. Otherwise, a serious mistake in media and spending levels could drastically affect the results.

2. A situation in which an example is available through research, association membership, or a competitive intelligence process. It is especially important in such a case to verify the information on which budget comparisons are made. As experience has proven, the initial budget and final actual spending might be dramatically different. Further, if the comparative model was executed in a significantly different geographic area, allowances should be made for differences in media and production costs.

Per-Unit or Percentage-of-Sales Method

In banking, a guideline that has been used to establish annual marketing budgets is to calculate expenditures as a percentage of assets. This method can be extended to a particular campaign by taking a percentage of either deposits or assets that are expected to be generated from the new product. Depending on the source, recommendations of 2 percent to 5 percent have been discussed. Generally, a new product will require heavier promotion up front, so the higher end of the scale should be considered.

Another way to calculate a budget from this method is to develop a detailed profit analysis and take a percentage of incremental profits that are projected during the first year or two of the product's life. (Formulas for measuring profitability can be found in Chapter 5.) The theory behind this method is that you can decide how much of the projected incremental profit to spend and how much to keep. The problem is that attempting to keep too much of the incremental profit will result in underspending which, in turn, may well result in not achieving the volume objectives.

Budget setting in this manner can become a very arbitrary process and, of all the processes, will most often result in a budget that is too low. This method is best suited to highly targeted programs in which the media mix is likely to be weighted heavily toward direct mail and sales promotion.

Task Method

By far, the most-preferred method of establishing a budget the task method. In this method, determining what activities are necessary to fulfill the objectives and determining the cost of those activities becomes the budget. In other words, the plan elements diagrammed in Exhibit 7.1 are used to determine the level that is necessary for each activity and that level of each element of the communication mix is budgeted for.

As an example, if the objective is to broadly introduce a new service to a wide cross-section of the marketplace, the media strategy might be to reach (R) 90 percent of the target audience an average of five times—frequency (F). That will require 450 gross rating points (GRP), or (R x F = GRPs). A combination of mass media that delivers the 450 GRPs will determine the media budget.

If the task is utilizing a more-targeted strategy such as direct mail to a selected list of several thousands consumers, a cost per thousand for the mailing becomes the budget figure.

These optimum budgets can then be fed back through the payback analysis process described in Chapter 5 to ensure that the expenditure is financially feasible.

The essence of this budget method is in the original objectives. The process is to determine what it would take to optimally accomplish the objectives and then cut back as necessary. In this way, what is being given up in the cut back and the effect these reductions might have on results is readily known.

Internal/External Implementation of a Communication Plan

As the plan's implementation schedule is finalized, it takes two distinct directions: internal and external. While the internal audience (employees) is *addressed* first in terms of the timing of the introduction of the message, the external message and rollout plan are *developed* first. The external message is then communicated through training and motivation programs to employees prior to being introduced to the public.

This process is illustrated in Exhibit 7.2. Each component of Exhibit 7.2 can be further broken down into its own process. These processes will be reviewed individually in the balance of this chapter.

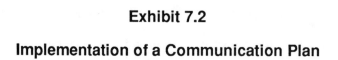

Exhibit 7.2

Implementation of a Communication Plan

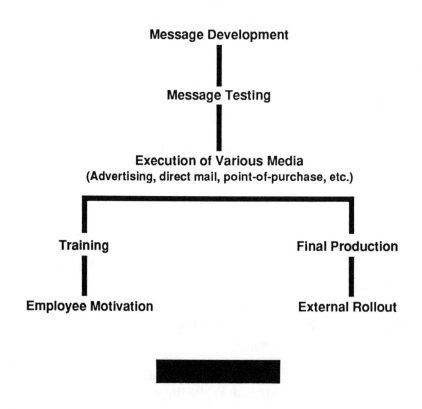

Internal/External Implementation of a Communication Plan

Message Development

There are any number of methods for organizing the creative process. Most marketing communication resources (advertising agencies, direct mail agencies, sales promotion houses, etc.) have a method they consider proprietary. In most cases, the method will have a unique twist of some sort. Whatever the process the support group uses, it should be measured against four basic criteria:

1. An in-depth definition of the target audience

2. Reading habits of consumers

3. A concise proposition to be presented to the target audience

4. An effective dramatization of the proposition in marketing communication

Defining the Target Audience: Information from market segmentation research done during the product development stage, discussed in Chapter 3, should be used to develop the marketing message. The needs identified in that research formed the basis for the design of the new product. The fulfillment of those needs must now be communicated to potential customers who have the need.

To ensure that the individuals who are executing the marketing communication plan fully and accurately understand the target audience, a written description should be prepared. This written description can be completed by the communication manager or supplier and presented as part of communication concept development. The information that follows should be presented to the advertising agency and then be included in their presentation back to you. This may appear to be a duplication of effort; however, it is an excellent method for verifying an understanding of the objectives and assuring that the ultimate creative solution is on target. The final written description should contain the following information:

- Target audience demographics—age, income, and geographic location

- Lifestyle characteristics—home value, types of automobiles, length of residence, and leisure activities

153

- Stage in financial life cycle—high-income/credit driven, accumulating, retired, etc.

- Specific needs to be addressed by the product being introduced

- Any other pertinent information gathered in the research phase

Reading Habits: Understanding the reading, viewing, and listening habits of consumers is very useful in selecting the right media mix for product communications. For example, FIMA/Raddon national research shows the different media habits of consumers. On average, consumers watch a total of 3.63 hours of television per day, listen to the radio on average 1.83 hours per day, and spend 23 minutes per day reading the newspaper (see Appendix B).

The Media Usage Research Tables in Appendix B show that these habits vary by age, account balances, income, and lifestyle clusters. Product research will assist an institution in identifying the "most likely customer profile" for the product, and then consumer research can be used to select the right media to target the product's message.

Reach and frequency can be controlled and directed in a most cost-efficient manner when the firm is committed to the importance of media research in successfully implementing products. Too often, a good product fails because the firm fails to effectively communicate the marketing message.

Developing a Concise Proposition to the Target Market: The concise proposition is a brief statement that distills the benefit to the customer into a one or two sentence statement. The statement is not meant to be, and should not be, an advertising headline or advertising copy. It should be a quid pro quo proposition to the potential customer.

Often, the proposition statement will begin with, "If you... " and end with, "You will receive... ". For example, "If you open one of our new accounts, you will receive... " (fulfillment of the need identified in the product development research)."

Some examples of proposition statements for various products might be:

- Home-equity line of credit

  "If you have an ABC Bank equity line of credit, you have instant access to cash by simply writing a check."

- Interest-bearing package account

  "If you keep $500 in a XYZ account, you receive free checking, money market interest, a no-fee credit card for the first year, and free traveler's checks."

- Consumer loan direct deposit

  "If you have an installment loan with XYZ Bank, you can reduce interest by 1/2% with direct-deposit checking and automatic loan payments."

This statement of the proposition should be written out and displayed during the review of actual advertising and promotion concepts, copy, and layout. The advertising message should then accurately reflect the proposition in a dramatic, attention-gaining fashion.

The proposition statement might also be called the positioning statement. The difference, however, is a tactical-versus-strategic orientation. The positioning of the product is inherent in product analysis and design while the proposition statement is a tactical tool utilized in the development of marketing communications.

In summary, the key to successful communication strategies is in developing a unique selling position that will clearly communicate benefits to the consumer and will successfully differentiate the product from thousands of other look-alike products. This is a significant challenge in an industry where most of the products are intangible, and difficult to differentiate. However, successful marketing people use research to build in a point of product difference and then direct the message at the market segments that have the highest propensity to perceive a high-level of product utility.

Dramatization of the Proposition: This is the actual delivery of the marketing message to the target audience in a dramatic though relevant manner—the actual advertising introduction of the new product. As mentioned earlier, this is the point at which good planning and excellent product design, based on an accurate assessment of need, can all go down the drain—and often does. The reason, of course, is that subjectivity takes over at the expense of logic.

There are two actions, however, that can be taken to prevent implementation of an advertising, direct response, or promotion that does not

155

accurately demonstrate the product's benefit. One action is to carefully follow the steps outlined above. The other is to develop at least two dramatizations to the extent that they can be tested through market research.

Message Testing

Message testing and measurement can be divided into three phases: Disaster check, diagnostic, and tracking. Depending on timing, complexity of the subject matter, and budget, any or all three phases might be used for a product's introduction.

Disaster-Check Phase: At the point that two or three promotional and advertising concepts have been developed, one or two carefully recruited focus groups can provide qualitative reactions to the message. These groups should be used only to recognize general perceptions and to identify broad categories of concern relative to the message being communicated.

The focus groups will tell if the intended message is being delivered, or if the concepts obviously miss the mark. The expense at this stage is minimal and well worth the time and effort. Many a brilliant and clever advertising theme has flopped because of some issue that would have been quickly identified by exposure to a handful of objective observers.

Diagnostic Phase: Once this qualitative research phase has been completed, it can be used to design a more quantitative and projectional piece of research. Not all programs will warrant this level of detail, but if significant media expenditure is planned, quantifiable copy testing may be a worthwhile investment to ensure maximum impact of the message.

Unlike product design, it is difficult to measure advertising in telephone surveys. A technique that is commonly used at this stage is the "mall intercept" or one-on-one interview process. In virtually every metropolitan area, there is a facility that can execute this type of research. Briefly, it consists of exposing individual consumers, who fit the target market demographics, to the advertising alternatives during a personal interview lasting fifteen to twenty-five minutes.

In these interviews, consumers are asked to discuss the main idea of the advertising, the product's details, the relevance of the message, their likes and dislikes, their opinion of the advertisements attention-gaining value, and their tendency to buy or not to buy. From this information, the final execution can be selected and modified through diagnostic analysis.

The Tracking Phase: Tracking consumers' awareness and recall of the advertising and promotion is a good measurement of effectiveness. Telephone surveys of a sample of the target market will provide data on the consumers' level of awareness of the advertising message. This information can be used to monitor and modify, as necessary, the media mix. Recall of the overall message as well as pertinent details by these respondents can provide feedback about the dramatization of the proposition and about its ability to compete with other advertising.

Exhibit 7.3 is a sample questionnaire used for tracking advertising and taking image/awareness measurements. The first three questions in the Main Questionnaire (the second page of Exhibit 7.3) deal with overall awareness of the institution and other institutions. The advertising questions, which are numbers four and five, measure awareness and recall of advertising. Questions six and seven deal with image characteristics. They should be asked to both aware and non-aware respondents, and compared to image profiles for competitive institutions. The balance of the questions provide demographic data on respondents.

All of these research techniques can provide useful, cost-effective data on which to base decisions about expenditures and to measure results. The discussion of them here has been purposefully brief for one reason. They should not be executed "in-house" unless a full-time experienced market research staff is available. Poorly executed, or misinterpreted, this information could be seriously misleading. A reputable marketing research firm or private consultant can provide reasonably priced support.

Execution of Various Media

Once content, dramatization, and testing of the message have been completed, the balance of the execution phase is simply managing the production process. At this point, the media plan should be completed and the media purchased. In fact, these things should have been done upon budget approval.

When the final date for the distribution of materials has been determined, due dates for each step in the production cycle should be developed. There should be two dates relating to each production step, a due date and an approval date. Time should be built into the schedule

Product Communication Strategy

EXHIBIT 7.3
SAMPLE ADVERTISING TRACKING STUDY
BANK CAMPAIGN MARKET MONITORING AND AD TRACK STUDIES

WAVE 1 [ ]
WAVE 2 [ ]
WAVE 3 [ ]
WAVE 4 [ ]

TEL. # _____

MALE   [ ]
FEMALE   [ ]

RESPONDENT NAME _____ ID # _____

ADDRESS _____ CITY _____

FOLLOW INSTRUCTIONS FOR RESPONDENT SELECTION AND RECORDING.

	ATTEMPTS		
	FIRST	SECOND	THIRD
DATE	____	____	____
TIME	____	____	____
BUSY (NA)	( )	( )	( )
INELIGIBLE	( )	( )	( )
OTHER (EXPLAIN)	____	____	____
COMPLETION	( ) .	( )	( )

(USE NEW SCREENER FOR EACH NUMBER ATTEMPTED)

Hello, my name is _____ and I'm calling for the Communications Teleservice, Inc. We're conducting a marketing research survey, and we would like to talk to the (man/lady) of the house. (VERIFY RESPONDENT CHOICE. CONTINUE OR MAKE CALLBACK APPOINTMENT). To qualify for this survey we need to know:

1.   Are you 21 or older?   Yes [ ] Continue No [ ] Thank. Terminate.

2.   Do you (or your spouse) have a savings or checking account?

Yes [ ] Go to main questionnaire
No   [ ] Thank. Terminate.

AN ELIGIBLE RESPONDENT IS A MALE OR FEMALE HEAD OF HOUSEHOLD, AGED 21 OR OLDER WITH A SAVINGS OR CHECKING ACCOUNT IN THE HOUSEHOLD.

CTI	BANK CAMPAIGN	WAVE 1 [ ]
	MARKET MONITORING AND	WAVE 2 [ ]
	AD TRACK STUDIES	WAVE 3 [ ]
		WAVE 4 [ ]

RESPONDENT NAME _____ ID # _____

MAIN QUESTIONNAIRE

1.   When you think of local financial institutions, which ones come to mind? (any others?)

2.   (FOR EACH INSTITUTION LISTED BUT NOT MENTIONED IN Q1, ASK) Have you ever heard of (BANK)? (START AT ✓).

(IF RESPONDENT IS UNAWARE OF BANK, SKIP TO CLASSIFICATION SECTION).

3.   If you were going to switch your primary savings or checking account today, which local financial institutions would you consider? (MULTIPLE ANSWERS)

4.   Which bank or banks advertising have you seen or heard in the past 4 weeks?

	Q1 Unaided Mentions First	Q1 Unaided Mentions Other	Q2 Aided Mentions	Q3 Consider Switch	Q4 Seen/Heard
Bank & Trust	[ ]	[ ]	[ ]	[ ]	[ ]
National Bank	[ ]	[ ]	[ ]	[ ]	[ ]
Savings Bank	[ ]	[ ]	[ ]	[ ]	[ ]
Colonial	[ ]	[ ]	[ ]	[ ]	[ ]
First Federal	[ ]	[ ]	[ ]	[ ]	[ ]
First Federal Savings & Loan	[ ]	[ ]	[ ]	[ ]	[ ]
Savings	[ ]	[ ]	[ ]	[ ]	[ ]
People	[ ]	[ ]	[ ]	[ ]	[ ]
Trust	[ ]	[ ]	[ ]	[ ]	[ ]
Other	[ ]	[ ]	[ ]	[ ]	[ ]
	_____	_____	X	_____	_____
	_____	_____	X	_____	_____
	_____	_____	X	_____	_____
None	[ ]	[ ]	[ ]	[ ]	[ ]

Product Communication Strategy

6.   Now, I'd like you to rate the Savings Bank on certain items. (START AT ITEM WITH ✓)
     Taking into consideration your experience with the bank, and what you have ever seen or
     heard about it, would you rate the bank as excellent, good, fair, or poor for (ITEM)
     (READ ENTIRE STATEMENT)

		EXCELLENT	GOOD	FAIR	POOR	DK/NA/R
( )	(Its) personal relations with its customers	[ ]	[ ]	[ ]	[ ]	[ ]
( )	(Having) convenient locations	[ ]	[ ]	[ ]	[ ]	[ ]
( )	(Being) open extra hours	[ ]	[ ]	[ ]	[ ]	[ ]
( )	(Being) helpful in all ways when needed	[ ]	[ ]	[ ]	[ ]	[ ]
( )	(Its) quality of service	[ ]	[ ]	[ ]	[ ]	[ ]
( )	(Its) service charges	[ ]	[ ]	[ ]	[ ]	[ ]
( )	(Its) variety of types of services	[ ]	[ ]	[ ]	[ ]	[ ]
( )	(Its) handling of small account customers	[ ]	[ ]	[ ]	[ ]	[ ]
( )	(Its) speed of service during peak hours	[ ]	[ ]	[ ]	[ ]	[ ]
( )	(Being) interested in people like yourself	[ ]	[ ]	[ ]	[ ]	[ ]
( )	(Having) friendly and knowledgeable employees	[ ]	[ ]	[ ]	[ ]	[ ]
( )	Caring about the community	[ ]	[ ]	[ ]	[ ]	[ ]

ALWAYS ASK LAST

( )	And, overall, how would you rate the bank	[ ]	[ ]	[ ]	[ ]	[ ]

7.   How familiar are you with the Savings Bank?
     (READ CHOICES)

        Very Familiar   [ ]
        Fairly Familiar   [ ]
        Not Very Familiar   [ ]
        Not At All Familiar   [ ]

--IF SAVINGS BANK MENTIONED IN Q 4, ASK Q5, a-e. OTHERWISE, SKIP TO Q6.

5a.   Thinking about the Savings Bank advertising you just mentioned, where did you see or hear it? (MULTIPLE ANSWERS ALLOWED)

Radio [ ]   TV [ ]   Newspaper [ ]
Other _____ [ ]_____ [ ]_____

5b.   What did the advertising say and show? _____

_____

_____

What else? _____

5c.   What was the bank trying to say about itself in this advertising? _____

_____

_____

What else? _____

5d.   Was there anything in this advertising that you thought was wrong, hard to believe, or that you disliked?

Yes [ ] Ask 5e
No [ ] Go to Q6
Not Sure [ ] Go to Q6

5e.   What was it? _____

_____

(PROBE . . . What else?) _____

_____

| ASK Q 6. |

9a. (IF SAVINGS BANK NOT MENTIONED AS "PRIMARY SOURCE" IN Q8a or 8b, ASK) Are you or anyone else in your immediate household now a Savings Bank customer for savings or checking?

Yes	[ ]		
No	[ ]	9b.	REPEAT FOR "EVER BEEN A
Not sure	[ ]		SAVINGS BANK CUSTOMER ..."

9b. REPEAT FOR "EVER BEEN A SAVINGS BANK CUSTOMER ..."

Yes   [ ]
No   [ ]
Not sure   [ ]

ASK EVERYONE

10a. Do you or anyone else in the household own or manage a business that uses banking services?

Yes   [ ]   No   [ ]   DK/NA/Etc.   [ ]

10b. And what is the name of that bank? _____

11. Are you . . .
    21 to 24   [ ]
    25 to 34   [ ]
    35 to 44   [ ]
    45 to 49   [ ]
    50 to 59   [ ]
    60+   [ ]
    Refused   [ ]

11a. Are you employed:
    Full-time   [ ]
    Part-time   [ ]
    Not employed   [ ]

12. Are you:
    Married   [ ]
    Single   [ ]
    Divorced   [ ]
    Widowed   [ ]

13. What was your total household income for 1986, before taxes (READ CHOICES)
    Under $25,000   [ ]
    $25,000-$34,999   [ ]
    $35,000-$49,999   [ ]
    $50,000 +   [ ]
    Refused   [ ]

14. Including yourself, how many people live in your household now? _____

Thank you very much for your time and your opinions.
STAPLE SCREENER AND MAIN QUESTIONNAIRE. RECORD RESPONDENT NAME ON BOTH.

CLASSIFICATION SECTION

ASK EVERYONE

8.   Now, for statistical purposes only, which of these personal, non-business financial services do you or anyone else in your immediate household now have or use? (CHECK IF YES)

a.   Checking account [ ]   How many? _____
     Primary source _____   and about how long has _____
     been your primary source _____?

b.   Savings account [ ]   How many? _____
     Primary source _____   and about how long has _____
     been your primary source _____?

c.   Credit card   [ ]

d.   Home mortgage   [ ]

e.   (Other) loans   [ ]

f.   IRA   [ ]   How many IRA's do you have?_____

g.   Private retirement plan
     (Non-employer sponsored) [ ]

h.   Money market or
     savings certificate   [ ]

i.   Certificates of deposits (CD) [ ]

j.   Travelers checks   [ ]

k.   Trust   [ ]

l.   Property-casualty
     insurance   [ ]

m.   Life insurance   [ ]

n.   Stock, securities brokerage [ ]

o.   Tax preparation assistance [ ]

p.   Safety deposit box   [ ]

q.   Reserve credit for overdraft
     checking   [ ]

163

to allow for revisions. A typical production schedule for printed material with realistic dates is provided in Exhibit 7.4.

Exhibit 7.4

Production Schedule Example

	Due Date	Approval Date
Copy/comprehensive layout	June 1	June 10
Mechanical production	June 25	June 30
Pasteup		
Separations		
Negatives		
Veloxes		
Etc.		
Release to media or printer	July 1	
Printer's proofs	July 10	July 15
Printing	August 1	
Internal/employee distribution	August 5	
External distribution	August 15	

Internal Communications

There is a ten-day delay between internal and external distribution. This delay provides time for orienting and training employees so that they become aware of the new product prior to its introduction to the public. The internal communication phase is probably one of the most important in the entire process. Without employees who are fully informed and in fact fully sold, the program has little chance for success.

Communications for employees can be written, videotaped, or passed down through management. The best method, however, is group presentations, where employees participate in a sales-training atmosphere. This allows for interaction and immediate responses to the reactions of others. The group method also reinforces the positive reaction and gives the trainer an opportunity to address any negative issues that may arise.

Employees should receive advance notice about the training, including time, place, how much time to set aside, a summary of the marketing plan, and instructions for preparing for the training.

The actual training should include the following:

- An explanation of the marketing situation and the marketplace's need that the new product will fill

- A summary of the product's development process and rationale for the product's design

- Operations instructions

- The marketing proposition

- The marketing communication theme and a brief overview of the message testing

- A sample of advertising and collateral materials

- The media plan and promotional timing

- Sales training—how to present sales points

- A sample of communications about the new product—See Exhibit 7.5 for a variety of communication devices used in rolling out new products

Summary

An understanding of the product communication process begins with the objectives, strategies, and plans in Exhibit 7.1. However, the heart of the process is the message development phase, where the product's target market and primary benefits are clearly articulated before any message is executed.

With clear, measurable objectives, an understanding of the target market, and a clear proposition, effective communications become a by-product of the process. The keys to the objective-setting process can be summarized in three categories:

Product Communication Strategy

- Understanding the market
- Accurate assessment of the new product's market potential
- Definitive determination of the factors affecting the ability to reach that potential

If these three categories are clearly understood, then clear objectives will emerge.

Understanding the market means that advertising personnel and communications agencies have an in-depth exposure to research findings on market segmentation. The objectives of each section of the plan—advertising, sales promotions, public relations, and training—should reflect this research and contain specific behaviors and attitudes that marketing should produce in the target audience.

An accurate assessment of the new product's market potential means that a clear definition of the total market is necessary, as well as accurate data on the market share of all competitors. Only with this information can a volume projection be determined.

The factors affecting the ability to reach maximum potential will vary depending on the sophistication of the targeted market segment and the complexity of the product. For example, a complex product may have an advertising objective of creating awareness and bringing potential customers into the bank. The training objective should then stress a high level of product knowledge and sales skills. A less-complex product, on the other hand, might have as an advertising objective to fully explain and pre-sell a product. The employee training objective in this case is to inform and prepare the employee for servicing the new product.

The strategies for achieving the objectives in each category of the communication mix are again dependent on the targeted market segments. For example, a mass-market checking product might have an advertising objective of introducing a product to a large percentage of the population in a short period of time. The strategy might then be to use prime-time television supported by the most-popular local radio station. An upscale line of credit, on the other hand, might use an advertising strategy that employs direct mail and telemarketing to selected neighborhoods, based on demographics and supported by newspaper or local magazine advertising.

Budget preparation has as a goal spending enough to get the job done, without spending more than is necessary. There are three budget-setting methods that can be used to determine the appropriate level of spending: historical method; per-unit or percentage-of-sales method; and task method.

Message development should be based on an in-depth definition of the target audience. To ensure that the individuals who are executing the marketing communication plan fully and accurately understand the target audience a written description should be prepared.

The key to successful communication strategies is in developing a concise proposition to the target market. The concise proposition is a brief statement that distills the benefit to the target customer in a one or two sentence statement.

The dramatization of the proposition is the actual delivery of the marketing message to the target audience in a dramatic though relevant manner.

Once the message has been developed, research should be implemented to better understand both message and media. Message testing and measurement can be divided into three phases: disaster check, diagnostic and testing. Depending on timing, complexity of the subject matter, and budget, any or all three phases might be used for a product's introduction.

Once content, dramatization and testing of the message have been completed, the balance of the execution phase lies in managing both the production process and internal communications.

Exhibit 7.5

Sample Communication Pieces

Introducing

A First Rate IRA With A Second Rate Option.

Norwest Banks proudly introduce a unique new IRA investment. The Trade-A-Rate Certificate. The most flexible IRA of its kind. With Trade-A-Rate, you get the option to "trade-up" to a higher rate once during the term of your certificate should Norwest Bank certificate rates increase. You choose the term—anywhere from 24 to 60 months.

Trade-A-Rate gives you more flexibility than traditional certificates. Plus a higher initial savings rate than many banks' short term or liquid IRA investments. And, of course, your money is FDIC insured.

> **Current Rate 7%**
> compounded annualy
> 60 month term/$1,000 minimum deposit

Call our Convenience Banking Center
291-BANK

We Know The Way. We Are Norwest.

NORWEST BANKS

171

REAL ESTATE

Our new Performance Mortgage lets you lock in today's low rates.

Only Yankee Bank's innovative new Performance Mortgage offers qualified applicants this unique two-step rate protection against today's fluctuating interest rates. First, Yankee Bank gives you the chance to lock in the rate at the time of application. So you don't have to worry about interest rates rising after you've signed on.

But what if interest rates should fall after you've locked them in? Yankee Bank protects you there, too. We'll review your loan seven days before closing, and if rates are lower at that time, you will automatically receive the lower rate.

You're protected if interest rates should rise – and yet free to take advantage if they fall. That's performance. And along with fast commitments, fast closings and competitive rates, that's what you get from Yankee Bank. Performance Mortgage loans are available in amounts up to $153,100 for both purchase and refinance, and in 15 or 30 year terms. Call Yankee Bank today at 723-1600 ext. 180 to find out more.

And unlock them later.

Yankee Bank
for Finance & Savings FSB

69 Tremont Street, Boston, MA 02108, 723-1600

172

A Quarterly Newsletter for IRA Clients

| Vol. 1, No. 1 Inaugural Edition | Winter 1986 |

Five Options Available

Home Federal Introduces Investor's Choice IRA

Our new, diversified Investor's Choice IRA is designed to help you build an IRA portfolio, using a range of investment options. We have five major options to choose from:

Fixed Rate Options

Terms:
- 12-18 month
- 18-30 month
- 30-48 month
- 4-10 year

Features:
- Fixed rate over the term.
- $50 minimum to open.
- 12-18 month account accepts additions (any amount).
- Higher rates for deposits/transfers/rollovers of $2,000, $10,000, $20,000.
- Choose any term from 1-10 years.

Money Market Options

Terms:
- Money Market (no term)
- 18-30 month
- 30-48 month
- 4-10 year

Features:
- Rate changes monthly with market rates.
- $50 minimum to open.
- All accounts accept additions (any amount).
- Higher rates for deposits/transfers/rollovers of $2,000, $10,000, $20,000.
- Choose from an account with no fixed term or select any term from 18 months to 10 years.

Guaranteed Return Options

Terms:
- Normally, 4- to 10-year Investments

Features:
- Fixed rate over the term.
- $500 minimum to open.
- Choose from three accounts, guaranteed to increase original deposit by 50% double or triple.

Discount Brokerage Option

Investments:
- Stocks
- Government securities (T-bills, notes, bonds)
- Corporate bonds
- Zero-coupon bonds

Features:
- Save up to 70% over full-cost brokerage commissions.
- Trades settled automatically through Home Federal Money Market IRA.
- Toll-free number for trades, market information and account information.
- Through Fidelity Brokerage Services, Inc., the nation's second largest discount broker.

- Unit investment trusts
- Covered options

Mutual Funds Option (Dreyfus-managed Funds)

Funds:
- Special Income Fund
- Aggressive Growth Fund
- A Bonds Plus Fund
- GNMA Fund

Features:
- No sales load or redemption fees.
- Ability to transfer money back and forth between your Home Federal Money Market IRA and your Dreyfus-managed mutual fund by telephone.
- Toll-free numbers for purchases and redemptions, fund and account information.
- $750 minimum to open, $500 minimum for additions.

Use of the Discount Brokerage Option or Mutual Funds Option, individually or with any other Option, carries a $25 set-up fee and a $25 annual trustee fee (per IRA Plan). Certificate, Money Market and GRO Options carry a $7.50 annual trustee fee (per IRA Plan).

Welcome to the IRAdvisor

1986 marks a new era for IRAs at Home Federal. A new, more diversified IRA, the Investor's Choice IRA. is now available to Home Federal clients! To go along with our new IRA, we introduce our new quarterly newsletter, *IRAdvisor*, written especially for our IRA clients.

In *IRAdvisor*, you'll find information on the latest enhancements available with your Home Federal IRA, in-depth discussions of the various IRA investment options, ideas for IRA portfolio creation and management, retirement planning strategies, tax law updates and information on other tax-advantaged products.

We hope you will find *IRAdvisor* to be a valuable addition to your Home Federal Investor's Choice IRA.

Cragin opens the door to new mortgage opportunities

Count on Cragin for innovative mortgage loan ideas that unlock easier, more accessible loan possibilities.

Following are brief descriptions of three exciting new Cragin ideas. For full details on rates, terms, etc., call any one of our five Regional Lending Centers: Chicago, 889-3230; Schaumburg, 884-0100; Mt. Prospect, 437-7850; Wheaton, 668-3600; Itasca, 773-0800.

New! The Cragin Short-Timer's Fixed-Rate mortgage

Here's a mortgage loan ideal for transferees or people who don't plan on owning their new homes more than five years. Yet, even if you're *not* in one of those situations, it still might be the best kind of loan for you.

9.00%

9.906%*

Annual percentage rate

Here's how it works: Cragin extends this mortgage to you at an unusually attractive interest rate. This rate remains constant for the 5-year term of the loan. The short term notwithstanding, your monthly payments remain low because they're based on the amortization of a 30-year term. What's more, there's no penalty for pre-payment.

If, at the end of 5 years, your home isn't sold, don't worry. Cragin guarantees to reissue a mortgage at the prevailing rates and terms.**

Indeed, you can choose any fixed-rate or adjustable rate mortgage Cragin has available at the time.

* Based on $50,000 loan, 3% closing costs and $250 application fee. Rates as of 11/17/86.
** Subject to standard underwriting requirements.

New! The Quick-Close AML, with 30-day closing — guaranteed

Cragin is open-minded when it comes to understanding that homebuyers are very closing-minded. So we invented the Quick-

Close Adjustable Mortgage Loan. This virtually unprecedented plan allows customers buying single-family detached homes to get the fast action they want. First, Cragin promises to give applicants a decision regarding approval within 7 working days. Next, after the buyer has selected one of our three AML options (with first-year rates as low as 7.75%),.Cragin commits to a closing date no further away than 30 days after initial application. And there are *no points* to pay at closing! Instead, you can defer closing points and pay them on a monthly basis over a 2-year period. It's a breakthrough idea developed by Cragin to help you break through red tape.

The Luxury Home mortgage — borrow up to $500,000 at regular rates

When you need a big loan, you need an S&L with the will and the wherewithal to finance it. That's Cragin. As one of America's largest S&Ls, we can offer loans up to a half a million dollars at the same rates you'd pay for a more modest home. And you've got the full choice of fixed-rate and adjustable-rate programs to select from.

The CD with rates that can easily glide upward, but can never slide downward

Cragin's revolutionary 2-year Safeguard CD

Too often today's saver has to play guessing games with unsteady interest rates.

"Should I lock into a long-term CD just in case interest rates go down?" some savers speculate.

"Maybe I should go into a short-term CD on the bet that interest rates will shortly rise and I can renew at higher interest later?" others guess.

Guess what! Cragin has taken the guesswork out of CD investment, with the breakthrough Safeguard CD. Here's how you're safeguarded against the rate rollercoaster.

First of all, Cragin guarantees your interest rate will *never be lower* than the rate on the day you open your account. However, every six months Cragin reviews your rate. And if 6-month CD rates rise, so does your interest rate. If they happen to slide, no problem. You still maintain your original rate. In fact, once your rate rises above the opening rate, it cannot go lower than your new, *higher* rate. In short,

there's no downside to a Safeguard CD, only an upside!

Free gift, too

But that's not all! As in the case of our regular CDs, your money is fully insured up to $100,000 by the FSLIC, *and* you can select a gift from our listings on pages 4 and 5.

Plus, we offer an affordable minimum deposit of just $5,000, and Cragin's solid 6-month rate to start.

Call the nearest Cragin office for current interest rates and all the details, now.

TAX-FREE INCOME
TAX-FREE GROWTH
TAX-FREE SECURITY

INVESTMENT SERVICES FOR AMERICA
IN/EST™
A SERVICE OF
ISFA CORPORATION
MEMBER SIPC

At

GreatAmerican Federal Savings®

50 YEARS 1934-1984

3 INVEST CENTERS

INVEST	INVEST	INVEST
1001 Lake Street	499 Lake-Cook Road	2122 22nd Street
Oak Park, Illinois 60301	Deerfield, Illinois 60515	Oak Brook, Illinois 60521
383-4078	564-2170	627-3860

MEMBER FSLIC

 **Kemper** GROUP

NAME _____

ADDRESS _____

CITY _____

STATE _____ ZIP _____

BUSINESS REPLY MAIL
FIRST CLASS   PERMIT NO. 729   OAK PARK, IL

POSTAGE WILL BE PAID BY ADDRESSEE

INVESTMENT SERVICES FOR AMERICA
IN/EST
A SERVICE OF
ISFA CORPORATION
MEMBER SIPC

At

GreatAmerican Federal
1001 Lake St.
Oak Park, IL 60301

NO POSTAGE
NECESSARY
IF MAILED
IN THE
UNITED STATES

Sample Communication Pieces

...The Kemper Tax-Exempt <u>Insured</u> Income Trust.

Now, at GreatAmerican Federal Savings you can get the quality products <u>and</u> the benefits of tax-exempt income through INVEST, the independent brokerage service of ISFA Corporation. Tax-exempt income is now easily available to everyone at GreatAmerican Federal Savings through the INVEST brokerage service. Every penny of income you receive is free from Federal income tax.* And you <u>don't</u> need $10,000 or $25,000 to start!

It's Insured: This is special—a tax-exempt income trust that insures** both interest and principal payouts will be made when due. As a result of such insurance, Standard & Poor's Corporation has given the Trust's Units its highest rating..."AAA"***.

It's Diversified: Kemper Tax-Exempt Insured Income Trust is an insured portfolio of long term, tax-exempt municipal securities, diversified geographically and by type of issuer and purpose. The result is increased protection for your investment.

It's Affordable: The minimum investment is $1,000.

It's Flexible: You can choose to receive cash distributions monthly, quarterly or semiannually or you can choose two ways to have your income reinvested for more tax-free income.

It's Liquid: Anytime you need money, you can redeem all or a portion of your investment at the then current net asset value, which may be more or less than you originally paid, and get same day pricing.

*Income may be subject to state and local taxes.
**The terms of insurance and reinsurance are more fully described in the Trust's prospectus. Neither the insurance nor the reinsurance removes market risk since they do not guarantee the market value of the Trust Units. No representation is made as to any insurer's or reinsurer's ability to meet its commitments.
***The "AAA" rating of the Units results from the insurance and reinsurance which relates only to the Bonds in the portfolio and not to the Units of the Trust.

- -

Send for a prospectus, containing more complete information, including fees and expenses, on Kemper Tax-Exempt Insured Income Trust. <u>READ IT CAREFULLY BEFORE YOU INVEST OR SEND MONEY</u>.

Name_____

Address_____

City_____

State & Zip_____

Telephone_____

FIRST
NATIONAL BANK
OF SANDWICH
MEMBER FIRST UNION BANCORPORATION INC

202 INDIAN SPRINGS CENTER
ROUTE 34 BETWEEN SANDWICH & PLANO
SANDWICH, IL 60548
815/786-8455

MEMBER FDIC

A Checking Account Plus a Whole Lot More!

FIRST FLIGHT CLUB I

Receive all these benefits FREE when you maintain a $100 minimum balance, or pay $7.00 a month if your balance falls below that amount.

UNLIMITED CHECKING

There's never a variable service charge for you as a First Flight Club member, regardless of your balance or the number of checks you write.

FREE FIRST ORDER OF PERSONALIZED CHECKS

As a First Flight Club member, you'll receive your first order of personalized First Flight Club checks at no charge.

ACCIDENTAL DEATH INSURANCE

Your First Flight Club I membership provides you with $5,000 in accidental death insurance through Continental Casualty Co. **NOTE: Coverage reduces by half at age 70 and coverage is divided equally among joint account holders.**

MONEY-SAVING DISCOUNTS

Every year, First Flight Club members are eligible to receive a pocket-sized Member Benefits book full of hundreds of discount offers. Inside you'll find valuable savings at hotels and motels across the country, auto rental companies, theme parks, entertainment centers, restaurants, campgrounds, special tour packages, and more!

CLUBMATE NEWSLETTER

Because you're a member of the First Flight Club, you automatically receive Clubmate three times a year. Your subscription to this quality publication will help keep you up-to-date on the latest financial topics, from tips on managing your money to saving on your taxes.

INTEREST ON CHECKING

As a First Flight Club member, you receive 5¼% interest on your club checking account with just a $500 minimum balance requirement.

FREE CREDIT CARD PROTECTION

Your First Flight Club membership entitles you to free credit card protection for as long as you hold your club account. When your credit cards are registered through our service, one toll free phone call is all it takes to ensure that your card issuers are promptly notified in the event of theft or loss.

FREE KEY RING AND REGISTRATION SERVICE

No more worry about lost keys! Your First Flight Club membership entitles you to a handsome, sturdy key ring with a special identification number. Should you lose your keys and the finder drops them into any mailbox, our national service center will promptly return them to you at no charge.

EMERGENCY CASH ADVANCE SERVICE

When you're out of town, out of cash and out of places to cash a check, your MasterCard or VISA can help you get the emergency cash you need in 30 minutes or less — nationwide — with Emergency Cash Advance. Simply dial our toll free number, 1-800-251-8597.

DIRECT DEPOSIT OF SOCIAL SECURITY CHECKS

If you receive monthly Social Security checks, we will arrange to have them sent directly to us from the Treasury Department for deposit into your account, with your authorization.

SYSTEMATIC SAVINGS

As a First Flight Club member, you're entitled to participate in our automatic savings plan. We'll transfer a predetermined amount from your First Flight Club checking account to your savings account on a specified date each month. And if you transfer at least $25 automatically with us, we'll put $5.00 in your savings account to get started.

NOTARY SERVICE

We'll notarize your signature without charge whenever you need the services of a notary public.

INDIVIDUAL RETIREMENT ACCOUNT

If you wish to open or transfer an IRA, we'll be happy to design a plan for you at no charge.

DISCOUNT BROKERAGE SERVICE

First Flight Club members can save up to 70% or more on brokerage commissions. If you make your own investment decisions, you can save money by placing your orders through our Discount Brokerage Service.

BANK-BY-MAIL

We give First Flight Club members all the deposit tickets and mailers they need at no extra charge.

MEMBERSHIP IN THE CLUB ASSOCIATION

All First Flight Club members receive numerous new services, local and national discounts, and benefits as they are added to the program throughout the year. Your membership card automatically identifies you as a member of The Club Association, a national association of club participants.

FIRST FLIGHT CLUB II

With no minimum balance requirement, you receive all the services of First Flight Club I, plus these additional benefits, for only $5.00 per month.

> **50% REDUCED MEMBERSHIP FOR FIRST FLIGHT CLUB II MEMBERS 55 OR OVER**
> If you are 55 or over, you receive all the benefits of a First Flight Club II account for only half the regular monthly membership fee!

5¼% INTEREST ON CHECKING

Your First Flight Club II account is a lot more than just a checking account because it earns 5¼% per annum interest on your entire balance.

FREE PERSONALIZED CHECKS

As a First Flight Club II member, you can forget paying for personalized checks. You'll receive all the First Flight Club checks you need at no extra charge.

ACCIDENTAL DEATH INSURANCE

First Flight Club II members receive accidental death coverage of $20,000 for death as a passenger on a scheduled airline and $10,000 for death by other accidents. **NOTE: Coverage (except for Scheduled Air) reduces by half at age 70 and is divided equally among holders of joint accounts.**

PREFERRED RATE ON CONSUMER AND HOME IMPROVEMENT LOANS

Receive First Flight Club's preferred discounted rate of ½% on your next consumer or home improvement loan! To qualify you must remain a First Flight Club II member in good standing for the life of the loan, and authorize us to deduct your loan payment automatically from your First Flight Club II account (keeping sufficient funds in your account for this automatic payment).

OVERDRAFT PROTECTION

No more overdraft charges for First Flight Club II members! If you overdraw your First Flight Club checking account, we'll automatically make a loan up to your personal line of credit. Ask us how you can qualify.

AND MORE!
- VISA traveler's checks, cashier's checks and money orders without issue charge
- 50% discount off first year's rental on safe deposit box
- Free photocopy service (limit of 3)

5/86

RADIO SCRIPT—NOW ACCOUNTS

(20 SECONDS OF NARRATION)

WHAT ABOUT THIS INTEREST ON CHECKING ... OR THE NOW ACCOUNT? ... IS THIS AVAILABLE AT MOST ALL FINANCIAL INSTITUTIONS? AND IS IT REALLY ALL IT'S CRACKED UP TO BE? IF YOU'VE BEEN WONDERING IF THIS NEW WRINKLE IN BANK-ING IS FOR YOU, STOP IN AT _____ AND ASK OUR PROFESSIONALS TO TELL YOU ALL ABOUT IT. COULD BE YOU'LL BE MONEY AHEAD.

###

Product Communication Strategy

██████████████████

October 6, 1986

John Doe Jane Doe
123 Maple Ave
Oakdale, OH 44441

TWO EXCLUSIVE BANKING SERVICES ARE RESERVED IN YOUR NAME.

I want to share with you some important news about two useful and
profitable, personal financial tools that have been expressly reserved
for Mutual's most credit worthy individuals — select individuals like
you who have earned special consideration.

First, it is my pleasure to offer you a <u>Free VIP Interest Checking Account</u>
for one year. The account, reserved exclusively for Mutual's mortgage
loan customers through December 31, 1986, currently pays 5 1/4% interest,
compounded monthly.

> There are no service fees. Or minimum balance
> requirements. <u>This alone can save you up to $96
> a year.</u> Additionally, you'll earn interest on the
> entire balance in your account.

And you save time and effort with Mutual's automatic loan payment
service, TRANSMATIC. Your payment is simply transferred from your
checking account on any day you choose — the 1st through the 15th of each
month. TRANSMATIC allows you to earn interest on your house payment until
the day it's transferred. You'll never worry about your payment being
late or lost in the mail.

Second, we offer you Personal Reserve — a very special credit line, at
Mutual's lowest rate. As of October 1, 1986, the rate was a low 7.50%.

> <u>And through December 31, 1986, I guarantee that
> the rate will stay at 7.50% or lower on your
> Personal Reserve Equity Line. If Mutual's prime
> rate falls, the rate you pay will too.</u>

After December 31st, the interest rate will change to a low 1 1/2% over
Mutual's prime. Based on the current rate, that's only 9.00% APR. Owner
occupied homes only.

You'll have instant access to the thousands of dollars in equity you've created with your regular Mutual mortgage payments. Personal Reserve will put from $5,000 to $75,000 or more — up to 85% of your home's value — at your immediate disposal. Plus the money to finance virtually any want or need — without disturbing your savings or other investments. What's more you'll have:

- No points to pay
- No application fee
- No annual fee for one year
- Free Personal Reserve checks

Here's how it works: You apply only once. Following approval, you'll enjoy checkbook access to your Personal Reserve. Use it as often as you wish, and for any purpose you feel worthwhile.

Remodel or redecorate... tuition... fund an investment... consolidate your credit card debts at a substantially lower rate... treat yourself to a vacation. You choose the reason and the amount. It's simple because your home secures the loan.

With Personal Reserve, you'll have the freedom to make these important financial decisions on the spot, with no additional approval required.

For your added convenience, Mutual has a full line of CDs and money market accounts with maturities ranging from 91 days to five years. Other loan services include car, boat, equity and personal loans.

For additional information on your Free VIP Checking Account, and to find out how much you qualify for with your Personal Reserve Equity Line, simply check the appropriate boxes on the reservation certificate and mail or bring it to your most-convenient Mutual office.

I know you'll want to take advantage of these valuable financial tools. They are just two of the easy banking services Mutual has designed to meet your changing financial needs.

Sincerely,

Samuel W. Hill
President

P.S. Having Free Interest Checking and a Personal Reserve Equity Line of Credit just makes good economic sense for the future. But this valuable offer expires December 31, 1986. So take advantage without delay.

181

VIP reservation certificate

John Doe
Jane Doe
123 Maple Ave
Oakdale, OH 44441

Let's talk more about:

☐ **FREE VIP INTEREST CHECKING**

☐ **PERSONAL RESERVE EQUITY LINE OF CREDIT**

Simply, return this certificate in the enclosed envelope. The manager of your preferred office location will call to answer your questions and make special VIP arrangements for opening your accounts. Offices are listed on the back for your convenience.

Telephone number: _____

Best hours to call: _____ A.M. _____ P.M.

Preferred office: _____

_____
(street address)

Or, if you have all the information you need, stop by, and present this certificate to open your accounts. Hurry! This exclusive offer is good only through December 31, 1986. We look forward to serving you and making banking easy.

Chapter 8

Case Studies in New Product Development

Market-Rate Passbook Case Study
Home-Equity Credit Products Case Study

Chapter 8

Case Studies in New Product Development

Market-Rate Passbook Case Study

General Background—
Regular Savings and Money Market Accounts

The regular savings account remains the most widely used deposit product. Three-fourths of all U.S. households have one or more savings accounts. In December 1982, deposits in regular savings accounts peaked at $358 billion.

The introduction of money market deposit accounts in December 1982 brought on a decline in regular savings account deposits. Deposits in money market accounts grew rapidly reaching $571 billion in early 1987.

In the lower-rate environment of 1986 and 1987, however, the regular savings account became a more-attractive product. Deposits in savings accounts rebounded from their low point in April 1984 and reached $387 billion in early 1987. It is apparent that the lower interest rate environment and the deregulation of interest rates on regular savings accounts has brought on a change in the product life cycle of the regular savings product.

Case Study Background

In this case study, the financial institution wanted to increase deposits. It was felt that the economic, regulatory, and competitive environment afforded an opportunity to market a product that was a hybrid of the regular savings passbook product and the money market deposit account—a market-rate passbook.

This case study discusses the various components that were used in the development of the product. Research data that was used to support the concept testing, target marketing, and segmentation strategies employed are included.

Legislative/Regulatory Environment

The Garn-St Germain Depository Institutions Act of 1982 authorized financial institutions to offer the money market deposit account. This account was designed to compete effectively with money market mutual funds. Money market mutual funds had grown rapidly after their introduction in 1972. They allowed the public to earn market rates in a liquid account.

Banks and savings institutions were bound by Regulation Q and could not effectively compete with this account. The legislation contained in Garn-St Germain removed the competitive advantage of money market mutual funds. Garn-St Germain also authorized a committee to phase out all existing regulations on interest rates and minimum balance requirements on deposit accounts offered by commercial banks and savings institutions.

On April 1, 1986, all the rate ceilings and minimum balances had been removed. The regular savings account, which had previously paid only 5-1/2 percent interest was now free to pay a market rate of interest. There were two opportunities presented by this final phase-out: raising interest rates on regular savings accounts to attract new customers, or removing minimum balances on money market accounts to attract customers.

Exhibit 8.1 shows some findings of a national consumer study on savings accounts. "Potential financial emergencies" and "I've always had one" were the two most important reasons cited for having a regular savings account. The study also yielded the following data:

- Passbook savings account holders were older and held higher liquid financial assets than statement savings account holders.

- Money market account holders were younger and had higher earnings than passbook savers.

- The savings account is a traditional rainy day reserve fund for most consumers. The affluent, though, use it as a minimum-balance accumulator.

Concept Testing

A focus group was conducted with a group of customers with high account balances. General findings were as follows:

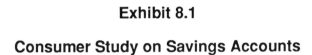

Exhibit 8.1

Consumer Study on Savings Accounts

Reasons for Keeping a Regular Savings Account	Total % Citing
"Potential financial emergencies"	37%
"I've always had one"	25%
"Convenient/easy to use"	16%
"Save for large purchases"	12%
"Accumulate money for other investments"	8%
"Safety"	4%
"I like passbooks"	3%

- Customers were extremely rate sensitive and would change institutions readily for a higher interest rate.

- The passbook provided a strong sense of security for older customers who had an inherent distrust of electronic technology.

- A high-rate or market-rate passbook account would be an extremely attractive product and would encourage customers to bring funds from other financial institutions.

- The market-rate product was so attractive that if a competitor were to offer the product, many of the focus group's participants would change institutions if it were not available at their current institution.

Quantitative Research: Estimating Demand

A quantitative telephone research survey was conducted with customers and noncustomers of the institution.

This survey sought to:

- Determine the demographics and lifestyles of customers and prospects

- Determine key market segments for targeting

- Determine market potential, product structure, and positioning for a market-rate passbook product

Some of the data, with implications for product development, from the survey is presented in Exhibits 8.2 through 8.6.

Exhibit 8.2

Customer Demographics: Age

| | | Market Area | | | |
| | | A | | B | |
Age	Total	Non-Customer	Customer	Non-Customer	Customer
18 to 24	8%	2%	1%	10%	9%
25 to 34	26%	26%	17%	30%	19%
35 to 44	26%	27%	17%	29%	19%
45 to 54	14%	16%	18%	12%	23%
55 to 64	11%	14%	27%	13%	12%
65+	16%	16%	20%	6%	19%
Total	100%	100%	100%	100%	100%
Average	44.8	45.7	51.9	40.0	46.1

Exhibit 8.3

Customer Demographics: Income

| | | Market Area | | | |
| | | A | | B | |
Income	Total	Non-Customer	Customer	Non-Customer	Customer
Less than $25K	22%	14%	10%	17%	20%
$25K to $50K	38%	46%	37%	42%	59%
$50K to $75K	14%	16%	4%	18%	7%
$75K +	8%	11%	4%	9%	4%
Refused	18%	13%	37%	14%	10%
Average $(000)	39.9	44.7	36.4	43.3	36.5

Exhibit 8.2 shows age data for customers and non-customers of the institution. Research for new products can focus on existing customers and potential customers. In this study, it was determined that the overall marketplace has an average age of 44.8 years. The study broke out two different market areas. Customers in each market area are older than non-customers in the same area. Market area A residents, in general, are older than residents of Market area B. Thus, market area differences could affect receptivity of the product if the product's potential is correlated with age.

Exhibit 8.3 compares income of customers and non-customers in Market areas A and B. The average income earned by survey respondents is $39,900. Non-customers in both Market areas A and B earn more than customers. The higher incomes of non-customers is an indication that potential for the product might be higher with non-customers.

Exhibit 8.4 estimates demand for the product if priced at two levels. Twenty-three percent of those surveyed indicated they they would be extremely likely or very likely to open a 6-1/4 percent savings account at their financial institution. Fifty-two percent indicated they would be not at all likely. The retired segment demonstrated the most interest in the product, with 40 percent being extremely likely or very likely to open the account.

Demand would pick up slightly if the minimum deposit were lowered to $2,000. However, 87 percent would still not open the account.

Exhibit 8.5 tests preference for a passbook or a statement with the product. Almost half (48%) of the likely users of the product would prefer a passbook. However, the high income percentage (36%) preferring a statement may indicate that the product should be offered with a statement option.

Exhibit 8.4

Product Demand and Pricing by Age

Question:

 If your financial institution offered a high rate savings account where you could earn 6-1/4% interest on deposits of $2,500 or more, how likely would you be to open one?

	Total	25 to 44	45 to 64	Retireds
Extremely likely	9%	8%	6%	14%
Very likely	14%	13%	17%	26%
Somewhat likely	23%	24%	23%	22%
Not at all likely	52%	54%	53%	38%

Question:

 Would you open the account if the minimum were $2,000? (Asked of those *not at all likely* to open account.)

	Total	25 to 44	45 to 64	Retireds
No	87%	86%	84%	71%

Exhibit 8.5

Passbook/Statement Preference by Age

Question:

With this market-rate account, would you prefer a balance register that you complete and a statement that keeps track of your balance mailed periodically to your home, or a passbook to keep track of your records?

	Total	Primary	25 to 44	45 to 64	Retireds
Passbook	48%	50%	46%	46%	60%
Statement	36%	34%	34%	37%	30%
Don't know	16%	16%	20%	17%	10%

Exhibit 8.6 evaluates the ability of the product to attract new customers. Overall, 28 percent of those who indicated they were at least somewhat likely to use the product elsewhere if it were not available at their institution.

Exhibit 8.6

Potential Loss of Business by Age

Question:

If a financial institution that you do not currently use were to offer this market-rate savings account and your institution did not, would you transfer funds to get this account? (Asked of those likely to open the account.)

	Total	Primary	25 to 44	45 to 64	Retired
Would change	28%	25%	36%	25%	38%
Would not change	38%	37%	34%	37%	31%
Don't know	34%	38%	30%	37%	31%

Case Studies in New Product Development

Business Plan

The business plan for the market-rate passbook addresses the basic decisions that need to be made. It maps out the product's features and the financial implications of various strategies for offering the product, including a special bonus promotion that was tied to the roll-out. The outline of the business plan follows:

I. New Product Strategy—Market Rate Passbook

    A. *Objectives*

        1. Lower long-term cost of funds

        2. Minimize interest-rate risk

        3. Build stable core deposit base

        4. Use opportunity to cross-sell other services

        5. Deter the run-off of regular savings to competitors

    B. *Product Features Promotion Strategy*

        1. Minimum balance: $1,000

        2. Passbook form

        3. Variable rate, indexed to MMDA rate

        4. Initial rate: 6.5 percent to 7.5 percent

        5. Promotional bonus of $100 cash

            a. Limited time only

            b. Deposit of $10,000 or more qualifies

            c. Bonus subject to rebate if account balance falls below $10,000 during the first year the account is opened.

            d. One bonus per household

            e. Ninety-day raincheck for payment of bonus if customer opens account for less than $10,000 and then increases balance to $10,000 or more within ninety-day period

6. Mass-media advertising in newspapers and occasional radio spots (Exhibit 8.7 contains two sample ads for the high-rate passbook.)

II. Strategic Approaches: Three Possible Scenarios

A. *Convert all savings accounts with balances over $1,000 to market-rate passbook account.*

1. Savings dollars in accounts with $1,000

"Golden" accounts (6%)	$ 7,063,350
"5-1/4%" accounts	$70,871,584
Total	$77,934,934

2. Increased cost of funds

a. 7.5 percent market-rate passbook

7.5% - 6.0% = 1.5% x $7,063,350 = $105,950
7.5% - 5.5% = 2.0% x $70,871,584 = $1,417,431
Total $1,523,381

b. 6.5 percent market rate passbook

6.5% - 6.0% = .5% x $7,063,350 = $35,316
6.5% - 5.5% = 1.0 x $70,871,584 = $708,715
Total $744,032

3. New dollars needed from outside to offset increase in cost of funds.

a. Earning asset yield—11.39 percent

b. 7.5 percent market-rate passbook

c. 11.39% - 7.5% = 3.89% spread
$1,523,381 ÷ 3.89% = $39,161,485

d. 6.5% market rate passbook

11.39% - 6.5% = 4.89% spread
$744,032 ÷ 4.89% = $15,215,378

Case Studies in New Product Development

Exhibit 8.7

LIMITED TIME ONLY!

Cash In On Your Age While You Get A Big Raise On Your Passbook Earnings

FRANKLIN PASSBOOK

Open Our Franklin Passbook And We'll Pay You Your Age In Interest – For Starters

Deposit just $1,000 or more in our new Franklin Passbook Account, and you'll earn 7.50% — a substantially higher rate than you've ever earned on a passbook. But that's not all. Open our Franklin Passbook right now, and, as a bonus we'll pay you your age — whatever it is — in interest for the first week on the first $1,000 you deposit, in addition to the 7.50%! If you're 60, that's 67.5% interest — if you're 95, that's 102.5% interest! (If Ben Franklin were alive today, he'd earn 286.50% interest).

You'll get all the convenience you're used to — total access to your money with no penalities, ever. And you'll have the peace of mind of watching your deposits, withdrawals and interest earnings recorded into your book right on the spot. Of course, your savings are protected to $100,000 by the FSLIC, an agency of the federal government.

So start earning a lot more on your passbook savings, as you cash in on your age. Open your Franklin Passbook Account today.

If Your Passbook Account Isn't Paying

7.50%

Call Us About Our Franklin Passbook

One Franklin Passbook age bonus per customer, please.

Since 1921

Ben Franklin $avings

MEMBER

FSLIC
Federal Savings & Loan Insurance Corp.
Your Savings Insured to $100,000

Oakbrook
Shopping Center
Oakbrook North Building
Oak Brook, IL 60521
Phone: 654-4770
Chicago Phone: 242-4036

Old Orchard
Shopping Center
61 Old Orchard
Skokie, IL 60077
Phone: 677-6150

Lakehurst
Convenience Center
Waukegan, IL 60085
Phone: 473-1300

7181 W. Irving Park Rd.
Chicago, IL 60634
Phone: 777-0800

196

Section 4   Chicago Tribune Monday January 6 1986

"A penny saved..."

is now a penny earning higher interest.

Introducing the Market Rate Passbook Account. The Northern Trust Company just made passbook savings a lot more interesting. Our Market Rate Passbook Account earns interest at rates that until now were available only on regular Money Market Deposit Accounts. Our current rate, guaranteed for thirty days, is 7.25%. The interest is compounded continuously from date of deposit and is paid quarterly.

Plus, you have unlimited access to your money and you can make withdrawals at any time without the interest penalties associated with time deposit accounts.*

To earn market rates of interest all you have to do is maintain an average quarterly balance of $1,000 or more. If your average quarterly balance drops below that you still earn 5½% interest and there is a $10 quarterly service fee.

If you prefer not to have a passbook, this account also is available with a quarterly statement.

Sound interesting? We'll show you how your hard-earned pennies can multiply even faster. Just call a Personal Banker at 630-6000 or visit any of our three locations in Chicago.

*You can make unlimited personal withdrawals but federal regulations require us to limit you to six preauthorized debits, automatic transfers, or telephone transfers to others in any one month.

Northern Trust Bank™
We want to talk, and you can quote us.

197

B. *Selective conversion of accounts with balances over $1,000 to market-rate accounts*

    1. Introduction of market rate accounts causes 20 percent of $1,000+ savings accounts to switch

"6%" money switching	$ 1,412,670.10
"5-1/2" money switching	$14,174,315.00
Total	$15,586,985.10

    2. Increased cost of funds

        a. 7.5 percent market-rate passbook

7.5% - 6.0% = 1.5% increase
1.5% x $1,412,670 = $21,190

7.5% - 5-1/2% = 2% increase
2.0% x $14,412,670 = $283,486

                    Total $304,676

        b. 6.5 percent market-rate passbook

6.5% - 6.0% = .5% increase
.5% x $1,412670.10 = $7,063.35

6.5% - 5.5% = 1.0% increase
1.0% x $14,174,315 = $141,743.15

                    Total $148,806.50

    3. New dollars needed to offset the increased cost of funds (case study institution's earning asset yield = 11.39%)

        a. 7.5 percent market rate passbook

11.39% - 7.5% = 3.89% spread
$304,676.35 ÷ 3.89 = $7,832,296.90

        b. 6.5 percent market rate passbook

11.39% - 6.5% = 4.89% spread
$148,806.50 ÷ 4.89% = $3,043,077.70

C. *Do not introduce market-rate passbook, competition offers similar product*

    1. With the introduction of competitor's product, 20 percent of the institutions accounts are lost to the other institution

    Funds lost

"6%" money		$1,412,670
"5-1/2%" money		$14,174,315
	Total	$15,586,985

    2. Decrease cost of funds

"6%" money		$84,760.21
"5-1/2%" money		$779,587.32
	Total	$864,347.53

    3. Cost of funds replacing lost funds

    8% x $15,586,985 = $1,246,958

    4. Increase in cost

    $1,246,958 - $864,347.53 = $382,611

    5. Opportunity cost of future earnings

    6. Goodwill/customer satisfaction lost

D. *Break-even balance requirement*

    1. Net-interest margin:

    11.39% - 7.5% = 3.89%

    2. Operating costs from Federal Reserve data = $36.44

    3. Break-even average balance

    36.44 ÷ 3.89% = $936

III. Product-line Positioning

Product	Minimum	Rate	Fees
5-1/2% (Statement)	None	5-1/2%	$2 if below $100
Market-rate (Passbook)	$1,000	Initial rate of 6.5% to 7.5% after—0.25% below MMDA (to be determined)	$5 if below $1,000
MMDA	$2,500	Varies	$5 if below $2,500

IV. Training Requirements

A. Minimum staff training is required with the market rate passbook because of its similarity to other existing products.

B. Meetings were held with customer-contact personnel to inform them of the operational aspects of the product.

C. A memo from the president to all employees informed them of the upcoming offering and promotion of the new product.

Conclusions

• The institution offered the market-rate passbook account with an initial rate of 7.5 percent.

• Advertising was done twice per week in the major metropolitan newspaper.

• The product attracted $120 million, with 65 percent of the deposits coming from outside the institution.

• The average customer who was attracted to the product was fifty-one years old, earned $35,400, and held liquid assets of $22,500.

• When the product reached maturity, in terms of growth, rates were slowly lowered and brought into line with the market. The institution has retained 80 percent of the product's peak deposit level.

Home-Equity Credit Products

Background

The Tax Reform Act of 1986 created an opportunity for rapid growth of the home-equity credit loan and line. This opportunity was created by the following elements of the act:

- The deduction for consumer loan interest expenses would be phased out over a period of several years.

- Homeowners would be able to use home equity to secure a tax-deductible second mortgage with the following conditions:

    — All equity in the home could be used for tax-deductible borrowing if funds were used for home improvements, medical expenses, or educational expenses.

    — The amount of equity that accumulated through the down payment, home improvements, and principal repayment could be used to secure a tax-deductible loan used for any purpose.

Current Consumer Credit Use

Exhibit 8.8 contains national data gathered by the FIMA/Raddon Strategic Research and Planning Program in the spring of 1987, on credit product usage.

Exhibit 8.8

Credit Product Usage

	Percent of U.S. Households Using the Product	Average Loan Balance
VISA Card	49%	$1,608
Mastercard	40%	$1,478
First mortgage	40%	$35,073
Auto loan	29%	$5,384
Personal credit line	20%	$495
Personal loan	15%	$5,053

EXHIBIT 8.9

Current Home Equity Use

Balance Level	% of Total	# of Households	% With Home Equity Product	# of Home Equity Households	Average Equity Outstanding
Less than $10K	46.8%	40,596,395	3/3%	1,339,681	$ 77,408
$10K - $25K	20.6%	17,869,353	6.6%	1,179,377	$ 32,015
$25K+	25.0%	21,686,109	3.9%	845,758	$126,667
Total Households				3,364,816	
Income Level					
Less than $25K	48.5%	42,071,050	1.4%	588,995	$ 15,500
$25K to $50K	33.1%	28,712,408	5.0%	1,435,620	$ 19,880
$50K +	14.4%	12,491,198	11.6%	1,448,979	$ 50,064
Total Households				3,473,594	
Area					
Midwest	25.8%	22,380,064	2.3%	514,741	$165,840
South	33.9%	29,406,363	3.2%	646,940	$ 97,983
East	21.3%	18,476,564	9.6%	1,773,750	$ 15,179
West	19.0%	16,481,442	3.6%	593,332	$122,100
Total Households			4.4%	3,528,763	$ 74,670

Small sample size leads to skewed distribution on outstandings.

According to Exhibit 8.8 credit-card holders and auto purchasers may be the greatest opportunities for the home-equity product.

Exhibit 8.9 shows that there are approximately 3.5 million households that currently use a home-equity credit product. The use of home-equity is greatest in the East. And middle-balance consumers use the product more often than do other demographic groups.

Questions were asked about the use of home-equity credit line and the amount of outstanding equity. Just over 4 percent reported using the product and they had equity balances averaging $47,670. Over half (57%) reported balances of less than $20,000.

Product Description

Loan Limit: Lenders will allow an individual to borrow up to 80 percent of the equity accumulated in the home. There are two ways of arriving at this credit-line amount.

	Method A				Method B	
	Home value	$100,000			Home value	$100,000
Less:	Mortgage owed	70,000			x Adjustment	80%
	Home equity	30,000				80,000
	x Adjustment	80%	Less:		Mortgage owed	70,000
	Credit limit	$24,000			Credit limit	$10,000

Method B is the more conservative of the two approaches currently in practice. It provides the institution greater insulation against declining home values.

Type of Loan: Two basic types of loans are available.

- Revolving lines of credit are loans that require monthly payments of interest only, or interest plus a small percentage of the outstanding loan balance. These loans have a term of from five to fifteen years and either rollover, convert to a fully amortized loan, or require a balloon payment at maturity.

- A fixed-payment, amortized loan has a term of between five and fifteen years.

Case Studies in New Product Development

Interest Rate: The majority of credit lines have variable rates of interest pegged at a certain percentage over the prime rate. Recent trends, however, have shown the emergence of fixed-rate, revolving loans with five year terms.

Product Development Task Force

The unique aspect of home-equity credit products requires involvement from more areas of the financial institution. The financial institution in this case study required involvement from the following areas.

Consumer Lending: Responsible for application taking, investigation of credit worthiness, and approval or denial.

Mortgage Servicing: Responsible for the day-to-day operations of outstanding home-equity loans, including data processing and consumer inquiries.

Mortgage Originations: Responsible for home-equity loan referrals, loan closings, and all associated paperwork.

Data Processing: Responsible for the design and implementation of all necessary mainframe programming, personal computer programming, and documentation.

Marketing: Responsible for product design, pricing structure, and product promotion, including direct mail and advertising.

Legal: Responsible for reviewing the current legal environment to determine if the product can be offered and under what terms; and for reviewing forms, including all documents, applications, and advertising to be sure they are in compliance.

Personnel/Training: Responsible for training all customer-contact employees on new product offerings, and specifically training customer-contact and mortgage originators on the fine points of the product.

Consumer Research

Consumer research was conducted to determine demand, key market segments, positioning, and features. The following highlights summarize the research findings and strategic conclusions for the product development task force.

Product Demand: Ten percent of homeowners indicated they would be extremely likely or very likely to take out a home-equity credit line. Local research showed that 72.8 percent of consumers in the marketplace are homeowners and that 103,895 of those homeowners would be extremely likely or very likely to use the product. Exhibit 8.10 illustrates how this number was determined.

This finding, while positive for the home-equity credit product, indicates that traditional forms of borrowing will remain more popular for the short run.

Exhibit 8.10

Demand Worksheet for Local Market

Households	1,500,000
Times 72.8% homeowners	1,092,000
Minus current users at 5.8%	63,336
Equals potential users	1,028,664
Times 10.1% extremely/very likely to use	103,895

Current Users	Potential New Users
63,336	103,895

Case Studies in New Product Development

Key Market Segments: Cross-sectional analysis of the research determined that the most-likely users had the following profile:

Age:	35 -54
Income:	$25,000 or more
Marital Status:	Married
Average home value:	$92,400
Average total equity:	$54,408
Average tax-deductible equity:	$17,408
Average amount they would borrow:	$14,600

Product Structure—Credit-Card Access: The research findings about marketing strategy for credit-card access with home-equity loans were as follows:

- Research findings: Only 5 percent of potential borrowers indicated that credit-card access would be extremely important with their home-equity loan, while 53% of potential borrowers indicated that they would not want their home-equity loan tied to a credit card.

- Marketing strategy: Development and promotion of credit-card access should be a low priority for the product because of low demand and possible adverse market reaction.

Product Structure—Home-Equity Loan versus Credit Line: The research findings and marketing strategy for home-equity credit products are as follows:

- Research Finding: Overall preference, as shown in Exhibit 8.11, was evenly divided between the home-equity credit line (revolving line of credit with a minimum payment each month) and loan (fixed monthly payment with specific loan life).

- Marketing Strategy: Given the increased demand for the product and the importance of tax reform, both to current and potential borrowers, a significant opportunity would be missed by not offering at least two products, a home-equity credit line and a home-equity loan.

EXHIBIT 8.11

Home-Equity Credit Product Preferences of Potential Users

	Line	Loan
Total potential users	50%	49%
Income		
Less than $25K	48%	52%
$25K to $50K	50%	50%
$50K or more	53%	45%

Product Positioning: The research findings and marketing strategies for positioning home-equity credit products are as follows:

- Research findings

    — Exhibit 8.12 shows that 58 percent of the time potential product users would use the home-equity credit product to remodel or improve their home. Thirty-eight percent of the time they would use the product in order to retain the tax deduction.

    — Low-balance holders were more likely to say that they would use the money for home improvements. High-income households were more likely to say that they would use the product to retain or obtain their tax deductions.

- Marketing Strategy:

    — From Exhibit 8.12 it is clear that two distinct market segments have emerged, home-improvement borrowers and tax-conscious borrowers. Previous studies have shown that the primary uses of equity lines were for home improvements and investments.

— Tax reform has created several important needs for the home-equity credit products, particularly among middle- and high-income groups.

Exhibit 8.12

Reasons for Using Home-Equity Credit

	Total	Equity Balance			Income		
		Less than $10K	$10K to $25K	$25K or More	Less than $25K	$25K to $50K	$50K or More
Remodel or improve home	58%	69%	49%	45%	74%	54%	47%
Retain tax deduction	38%	30%	49%	43%	24%	35%	61%
Finance car purchase	26%	25%	18%	31%	24%	23%	34%
Consolidate higher-cost loan	23%	29%	21%	17%	22%	28%	18%
Pay for educational expenses	20%	26%	21%	7%	20%	24%	11%
Pay for medical expenses	16%	19%	21%	5%	24%	16%	3%
Fund investments	13%	8%	10%	24%	4%	13%	24%
Emergency cash reserve	13%	16%	15%	7%	16%	13%	13%
Other	7%	7%	3%	10%	4%	9%	8%

Pricing/Profitability

Deciding on a pricing structure for home-equity credit line products has posed a significant challenge to the industry. The high cost associated with putting these loans on the books, consumer acceptance, and product complexity have made pricing this product extremely difficult.

To understand the interplay between the different components of home-equity pricing in the consumer's mind, a technique known as conjoint analysis is used. Conjoint analysis, which has been called "trade-off" analysis, allows an institution to examine a product's component parts and to measure consumer values for each specific component. With the information on consumer values, the market's reaction to new and existing products and services can be simulated.

The simulation of market reaction to a product gives a "preference share" for a product in terms of its market appeal. Using the preference share for a product and the profit margin on each alternative, an institution can make optimal decisions for pricing on earnings, market share, and competitive analysis.

For the home-equity credit line product, this case study sought to identify consumer values for four components of the home-equity credit line. The pricing components are rate, pricing total cost to obtain a loan, payment price, and annual fee.

Home-Equity Product Components

Rate	Total Cost to Obtain Loan	Payment Structure	Annual Fee
Prime	$0	Interest only	$0
Prime + 1	$200	P & I	$25
Prime + 2	$500		

Consumers were asked to rank the attractiveness of nine different home-equity credit line products with different combinations of levels for the four pricing features, as shown in the table above. Each rating tells something about how the respondent valued the four attribute levels, to one another.

Exhibit 8.13

Home-Equity Pricing Utilities

Rate	Utility	Approval costs	Utility
Prime	66.43	$0	79.14
Prime + 1/2%	49.77	$100	63.02
Prime + 1%	33.11	$200	46.96
Prime + 1-1/2%	16.93	$300	31.27
Prime + 2%	.74	$400	15.63
		$500	0

Interest Structure	Utility	Annual Fee	Utility
Interest only	24.77	$0	42.75
Principal & interest	1.88	$10	27.42
		$20	12.09
		$25	4.42

Once the analysis is completed the institution determined the values associated with each level and interpolated or estimated reactions to home-equity product configurations not specifically asked, but within the range of prices presented.

Exhibit 8.13 highlights the home-equity pricing utilities. These utilities give some immediate insights into the consumers values.

Closing costs have the highest utility to the consumer. A product with lower closing costs has greater utility than one with lower interest rate, if all other features of the product are equal. Specifically, consumers prefer a product with a rate of prime plus 2 percent, and no closing costs, to a product at prime rate with up-front costs of $500. Based on utilities, a 1/2 percent increase in the loan's interest rate is approximately equal to $100 of up-front loan fees. This same relationship is true even when it goes against the consumer's economic benefit. Those planning on borrowing $50,000 or more on their home-equity credit line still place a higher value on lower up-front costs than on a lower interest rate.

Example: Total Product Preference-Share Comparison

> In this example, respondents in the survey who indicated that they would borrow $50,000 or more on a home-equity credit line showed the following dollar share of preference for three loans.

	$50K+ Borrowers Share of Preference
Prime rate + 2% No up-front costs	81.4
Prime rate + 1% $200 up-front costs	90.6
Prime rate $500 up-front costs	69.6

> In this example the highest share of preference, or total utility, is achieved from the prime-plus-1 percent loan with $200 in up-front costs.

It should be noted that share of preference, or utility, cannot be directly related to market share in this study. In a real marketplace, many other variables, such as advertising, sales force effectiveness, and the financial institution's image, can interact with the ultimate decision. These other variables can be measured, and utilities estimated for them, if a specific market area is studied. An estimate of market share can be very helpful in pricing decisions.

Consumer Preference Simulation Model

Profit: When an institution has the utilities for each product component, it can create a model that can be used to make pricing decisions. Pricing decisions can be made for several situations:

1. Profit per loan maximization
2. Market share maximization
3. Reaction to competitive pricing
4. Total profit maximization

Case Studies in New Product Development

The following pricing components were used in this conjoint analysis:

- Payment structure and annual fee were not included in the initial analysis because of their lower utilities and their smaller impact on profit. They can be reinserted for product refinement after some of the many combinations have been eliminated.

- For profit purposes, the following assumptions were used:

  — Cost to originate loan: $500

  — (Cost/fees) amortized over life of loan

  — Life of loan: Five years

  — Average balance: $30,000

  — Prime rate: 7.5 percent

  — Cost of funds: 7 percent

While there can be many variations on these variables, it is important that the many variables be kept *constant* during the initial analysis.

In Exhibit 8.14, loans are grouped by profitability. Product preference varies considerable for similarly profitable loans. This example could be used when an institution is profit driven and cannot handle a large volume. Within the most profitable loan group, the institution should select the loan with the highest-product share preference.

Within loans providing a profit of $700 or more per loan, the product share preference varies from .74 to 47.64, a sixty-four fold difference. Prime, plus 2 percent, plus $200 closing, and application fees would maximize consumer preference share and profitability.

In Exhibit 8.15, grouping loans in descending preference-share order allows us to make two pricing decisions: pricing in reaction to competitors and pricing for maximum consumer attractiveness.

For example, the primary competitor's product is priced at prime, with $200 in up-front fees, another institution by pricing its loan at prime, plus 1/2 percent, with $100 in fees would be equally attractive to the marketplace and yield a profit per loan that is $130 higher.

EXHIBIT 8.14

Pricing Decision #1 - Profit Per Loan Maximization

Rate	Closing Costs	Product Share Preference	Annual Profit per Loan	Profit Index
Prime + 2%	$500	.74	$770	570
Prime + 2%	$400	16.37	$750	12,278
Prime + 2%	$300	32.01	$730	23,367
Prime + 2%	$200	47.64	$710	33,824
Prime + 2%	$100	63.76	$690	43,994
Prime + 2%	$ 0	79.88	$670	53,520
Prime + 1.5%	$500	16.93	$620	10,497
Prime + 1.5%	$400	32.56	$600	19,536
Prime + 1.5%	$300	48.20	$580	27,956
Prime + 1.5%	$200	63.83	$560	35,745
Prime + 1.5%	$100	79.95	$540	43,173
Prime + 1.5%	$ 0	96.07	$520	49,956
Prime + 1%	$500	33.11	$470	15,562
Prime + 1%	$400	48.74	$450	21,933
Prime + 1%	$300	64.38	$430	27,683
Prime + 1%	$200	80.01	$410	32,804
Prime + 1%	$100	96.13	$390	37,491
Prime + 1%	$ 0	112.25	$370	41,533
Prime + 1/2%	$500	49.77	$320	15,926
Prime + 1/2%	$400	65.40	$300	19,620
Prime + 1/2%	$300	81.04	$280	22,691
Prime + 1/2%	$200	96.67	$260	25,134
Prime + 1/2%	$100	112.79	$240	27,070
Prime + 1/2%	$ 0	128.91	$220	28,360
Prime	$500	66.43	$170	11,293
Prime	$400	82.06	$150	12,309
Prime	$300	97.70	$130	12,701
Prime	$200	113.33	$110	12,466
Prime	$100	129.45	$ 90	11,650
Prime	$ 0	145.57	$ 70	10,190

Case Studies in New Product Development

EXHIBIT 8.15

Pricing Decision #2 - Competitive
Pricing Decision #3 - Market Share Maximization

Rate	Closing Costs	Product Share Preference	Annual Profit per Loan	Profit Index
Prime	$ 0	145.57	$ 70	10,190
Prime	$100	129.45	$ 90	11,650
Prime + 1/2%	$ 0	128.91	$220	28,360
Prime	$200	113.33	$110	12,466
Prime + 1/2%	$100	112.79	$240	27,070
Prime + 1%	$ 0	112.25	$370	41,533
Prime	$300	97.70	$130	12,701
Prime + 1/2%	$200	96.67	$260	25,134
Prime + 1%	$100	96.13	$390	37,491
Prime + 1.5%	$ 0	96.07	$520	49,956
Prime	$400	82.06	$150	12,309
Prime + 1/2%	$300	81.04	$280	22,691
Prime + 1%	$200	80.01	$410	32,804
Prime + 1.5%	$100	79.95	$540	43,173
Prime + 2%	$ 0	79.88	$670	53,520
Prime	$500	66.43	$170	11,293
Prime + 1/2%	$400	65.40	$300	19,620
Prime + 1%	$300	64.38	$430	27,683
Prime + 1.5%	$200	63.83	$560	35,745
Prime + 2%	$100	63.76	$690	43,994
Prime + 1/2%	$500	49.77	$320	15,926
Prime + 1%	$400	48.74	$450	21,933
Prime + 1.5%	$300	48.20	$580	27,956
Prime + 2%	$200	47.64	$710	33,824
Prime + 1%	$500	33.11	$470	15,562
Prime + 1.5%	$400	32.56	$600	19,536
Prime + 2%	$300	32.01	$730	23,367
Prime + 1.5%	$500	16.93	$620	10,497
Prime + 2%	$400	16.37	$750	12,278
Prime + 2%	$500	.74	$770	570

Exhibit 8.16

Pricing Decision #4—Profit Maximization Estimation

Rate	Closing costs	Product Share Preference	Annual Profit per Loan	Profit Index
Prime + 2%	$0	79.88	$670	53,520
Prime + 1.5%	$0	96.07	$520	49,956
Prime + 2%	$100	63.76	$690	43,994
Prime + 1.5%	$100	79.95	$540	43,173
Prime + 1%	$0	112.25	$370	41,533
Prime + 1%	$100	96.13	$390	37,491
Prime + 1.5%	$200	63.83	$560	35,745
Prime + 2%	$200	47.64	$710	33,824
Prime + 1%	$200	80.01	$410	32,804
Prime + 1/2%	$0	128.91	$220	28,360
Prime + 1.5%	$300	48.30	$580	27,956
Prime + 1%	$300	64.38	$430	27,683
Prime + 1/2%	$100	112.79	$240	27,070
Prime + 1/2%	$200	96.67	$260	25,134
Prime + 2%	$300	32.01	$730	23,367
Prime + 1/2%	$300	81.04	$280	22,691
Prime + 1%	$400	48.74	$450	21,933
Prime + 1/2%	$400	65.40	$300	19,620
Prime + 1.5%	$400	32.56	$600	19,536
Prime + 1/2%	$500	49.77	$320	15,926
Prime + 1%	$500	33.11	$470	15,562
Prime	$300	97.70	$130	12,701
Prime	$200	113.33	$110	12,466
Prime	$400	82.06	$150	12,309
Prime + 2%	$400	16.37	$750	12,278
Prime	$100	129.45	$90	11,650
Prime	$500	66.43	$170	11,293
Prime + 1.5%	$500	16.93	$620	10,497
Prime	$0	145.57	$70	10,190
Prime + 2%	$500	.74	$770	570

If an institution wants to maximize market share, the top three loans should have similar consumer appeal. Prime, plus 1/2 percent, with no up-front costs is three-times more profitable than prime with no up-front costs.

In the profit maximization estimation, Exhibit 8.16 annual profit per loan ranges from $70 to $770. Product share preference ranges from .74 to 145.57. In general, profit per loan and product share preference are juxtaposed. The least-profitable loan has the most utility to the consumer, or product share preference, while the most-profitable loan is the least attractive to the consumer. To maximize profit in this mode, a profit index that multiplies profit per loan by product share preference is calculated.

It is important to remember that product share preference is an indication of value and may not be directly linked to market share. Other variables such as competition, image, and advertising also effect market share.

The loan that has the highest combination of preference, share, and annual profit is prime, plus 2 percent, and no up-front costs. Industry experience in highly competitive markets has shown, however, that waiving up-front costs will lower loan amounts and activation rates. In a competitive situation, therefore, prime, plus 2 percent, with $100 up-front costs may be more attractive to the institution.

Promotional Strategies

The following promotional strategies were recommended for the home-equities credit product:

1. Direct-mail solicitation of mortgage loan customers

2. Cross-sales to new mortgage applicants

3. Direct mail to noncustomer households

Exhibit 8.17 contains five samples of direct-mail and print-media ads for home-equity products.

Exhibit 8.17

*Samples of Direct-Mail and Print-Media Ads
for Home Equity Products*

Mr. Ramsey Demir
181 Millbrook Road
North Haven, CT   06518

RE: Connecticut HomeLine   SPECIAL NO FEE OFFER

Dear Mr. Demir:

At CBT, we recognize that your home equity is one of your most valuable assets. For several years, we've been helping homeowners put their home equity to work with Connecticut HomeLine. Connecticut HomeLine lines of credit have been used for many reasons, including home improvements, college tuition, consolidation of other loan payments, the purchase of cars and boats, and special investment opportunities.

Now, we've added a new special dimension to Connecticut HomeLine. And you, as one of our valued customers, can be among the first to take advantage of it.

> For a limited time only, we will absorb the attorney, appraisal, and application fees ordinarily associated with this type of account. These fees usually amount to $350 to $1,200 or more.

This special no-fee offer means that you pay nothing until you actually use the funds. When you do, you'll pay only an Annual Percentage Rate calculated on 1 1/2% above the Prime Rate published in The Wall Street Journal on our last business day of each month. Few personal loan rates are this attractive. And, because the Connecticut HomeLine interest rate changes each month that the Prime Rate changes, you can be sure that it's consistently one of the lowest rates available to an individual. The Annual Percentage Rate for January 1986 was only 11.15%. Call us toll-free, at 1-800-842-2295 and we'll be pleased to tell you today's Annual Percentage Rate.

We're prepared to process your Connecticut HomeLine application immediately, so that you can begin to enjoy the opportunities that Connecticut HomeLine can make possible. In fact, we're committed to giving you a decision on your application within five business days from the day we receive it. After your application is approved, you'll have your Connecticut HomeLine in two weeks, barring some unusual circumstance.

It costs you nothing to apply. And, it won't cost a thing until you actually use your Connecticut HomeLine funds. So take advantage of this special offer, and don't hesitate to call us if you need assistance completing your application.

Cordially,

Harry J. Drolet
Senior Vice President

Determine Your Potential Line of Credit With Connecticut HomeLine

Use this formula:

1. 80% of the current value of your home $ _____

    minus

2. The balance due on your existing mortgage   - $ _____

    equals

3. Your potential line of credit with Connecticut HomeLine   = $ _____

March 10, 1986

John Kamaras
Grassy Hl Rd
Orange CT 06477

Dear John Kamaras

How can you get up to $50,000 FREE
using the equity built up in your home?
It's easy. Just come to
Connecticut Savings Bank
right now for a free
Equity Line of Credit.

    NO POINTS
    NO CLOSING
    NO APPLICATION FEE
    NO ANNUAL MEMBERSHIP FEE
    NO COST OF ANY KIND EXCEPT INTEREST ON THE MONEY YOU BORROW

You can use the money for anything you want, just by writing a check. Buy a new car, a new boat, take a dream vacation or put the money towards home improvements. Whatever your dreams, we can help you make them come true.

But act now! This is a limited time offer. The enclosed brochure will give you all the details you need on how to set up a free Equity Credit Line. If you have other questions, stop by a local branch or call us at (203) 773-4567.

Sincerely,

Thomas W. Keefe, Vice President
Consumer Loan Division

P.S. This is a once-in-a-lifetime opportunity to use $50,000 FREE! And you don't have to have your mortgage with us to take advantage of it.

A LOAN FOR HOMEOWNERS WHO WANT TO KNOW EXACTLY WHAT THEY'RE GETTING INTO.

If you've been thinking about taking out a loan to put an addition on the house or to pay a college tuition or to buy something frivolous like a hot tub for the backyard, but you're not totally comfortable with the variable-rate home equity loans being offered by most banks today, relax.

Because at The Provident, we offer you an alternative: a Provident Second Mortgage.

It works like the other home equity loans – using the equity you have in your home as collateral. But a Provident Second Mortgage gives you a rate that's fixed for the full term of your loan.

With a Provident Second Mortgage you can borrow from $3,500 to over $100,000. You can choose from several terms with very competitive annual percentage rates: 10.95% for 5 years, 11.50% for 10 years or 11.95% for 15 years. And you pay *no points*, a *very low* closing fee, and *no penalty charge* if you decide to pay your loan off early.

So call us at 423-9600 for more information on how you can get a Provident Second Mortgage.

It could open the door to all kinds of possibilities.

The Lending Group at The Provident

Boston: 36 Temple Place (Headquarters), Charles River Plaza, 70 Federal St., 306 Hanover St., 43 Kneeland St., Prudential Center Plaza, 25 State St. Also: 423 Washington St., Brighto ugus Plaza, Saugus, 572 Freeport St., Dorchester

BayBanks offers homeowners something better.

With REAL Credit, you can get up to $100,000 or more with absolutely no fees.

Now you can turn the built-in equity in your Massachusetts home into ready cash—up to $100,000 or more.

Save $300.

Join the thousands of homeowners who have already opened a revolving line of credit with this special offer. You can open a revolving line of credit with no up-front costs when you have a BayBanks Money Manager Account," or a BayBanks checking, NOW, or Capital account. With this special REAL Credit offer, there are no application fees. No attorney's fees. No appraisal fees.*

Borrow at our best consumer rate.

REAL Credit costs nothing

until you use it. The interest rate is set monthly at only 1½% above the BayBanks Prime Rate. For example, the REAL Credit Annual Percentage Rate on August 25, 1986 was 9.50%.

Access your credit line by writing a check.

You can use REAL Credit anytime you want. And for any reason. Home improvement. College tuition. Medical expenses. Automobile. Vacation. Just write a check up to the amount of your available credit.

REAL Credit comes with something different—a choice.

With REAL Credit, you get a

book of special REAL Credit checks. That means you can access your credit line directly, without worrying about your checking account balances.

Or, if you prefer, you can get REAL Credit with a BayBanks Money Manager Account. So you'll have all your finances in a single, easy-to-manage account.

With REAL Credit, it really does keep getting better.

No one makes it easier than BayBanks. To apply for REAL Credit, or to get more information, stop by any of our more than 200 conveniently located offices. Or call one of our Customer Service Centers listed below.

BayBanks®

IT JUST KEEPS GETTING BETTER.™

Customer Service Centers:
BayBank Boston 648-8330, BayBank First Easthampton 586-8600, BayBank Harvard Trust 648-8330, BayBank Merrimack Valley 475-3620, BayBank Middlesex 387-1808, BayBank Norfolk Trust 461-1740, BayBank Southeast 1-800-447-6800, BayBank Valley Trust 781-7575.

*Our estimate of the value of your home will ᵇ̣ ₒased upon your most recent property tax bill. An appraisal fee will be applied if you request a new appraisal. Members FDIC.

223

Charge A Car

9.5%
Current Prime-Based Rate*

SCF CreditLine

With SCF CreditLine, You Can Still Deduct The Interest

Limited deductions for interest on car loans. That's the new tax law. And it doesn't stop there. Deductions on student loans, personal loans, regular credit cards, and lots of other traditional consumer credit are limited or out altogether.

But that doesn't mean your future deductions are out. All you need to keep deducting interest is SCF CreditLine. That's because the new law allows interest deductions on SCF CreditLine when it's secured by the equity in your home – so long as the amount you borrow doesn't exceed your home's original purchase price plus the cost of any improvements.

SCF CreditLine is not only the smartest way to borrow, it's the easiest. When a buying opportunity arises, just reach for your SCF CreditLine Gold MasterCard Card or special CreditLine checkbook.

Visit South Carolina Federal and apply for SCF CreditLine today. Before you know it, you'll be able to charge a car, a kitchen, or any important purchase – and deduct the interest.

If you hurry and apply before December 1, 1986, South Carolina Federal will pay all real estate closing costs and appraisal fees normally associated with a loan of this type. This can save you from $200 to $400 if you use the professionals participating in this offer. Of course, you may choose your own attorney at your expense.

South Carolina Federal

Member FSLIC. Accounts federally insured to $100,000.

*Normal credit standards apply. The interest rate on SCF CreditLine is variable, is valid for CreditLine accounts secured by real estate, and is subject to change without notice. The rate charged is based on the "prime rate" as published by the Wall Street Journal. Individual purchases with your SCF CreditLine account must be for at least $100.

Direct Mail Solicitation of Mortgage Loan Customers: The case study institution's direct-mail solicitations to noncustomers will focus on the targeted market demographics. Mailing lists will be bought at the block group level in areas with concentrations of the following types of individuals:

Age:	35-54
Income:	$25K+
Length of residence:	5 years
Home value:	$75,000+

It is anticipated that a response rate of 12 percent can be achieved. Based on that estimate, mailings will be staggered to control the volume of applicants.

Cross-Sales to Mortgage Applicants: National consumer research done by the FIMA/Raddon Strategic Research and Planning Program during the fall of 1986 determined that there is a significant opportunity to cross-sell home-equity credit lines to new mortgage applicants who make qualifying down payments.

The following was asked of recent mortgage applicants:

Some mortgage lenders are offering a home-equity credit line with their mortgage *for no additional fee.* This is a revolving line of credit that allows you to borrow up to $25,000 for any purpose you choose. Funds are accessed by check. The rate is adjusted to the prime business rate and is currently between 9 percent and 11 percent. How likely would you be to use this loan?

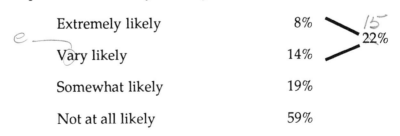

Extremely likely	8%
Vary likely	14%
Somewhat likely	19%
Not at all likely	59%

If offered a home-equity credit line with no additional fees, or points, at the time of taking out a mortgage, almost one-fourth of the mortgage applicants would accept the loan.

Case Studies in New Product Development

The experience of three institutions supports this cross-selling strategy.

1. A northeastern institution offered four types of mortgages to applicants. One of the options include a home-equity credit line at no additional cost. Approximately one-fourth of all mortgage applicants selected the option with the home-equity credit line.

2. A midwestern institution turned over all approved mortgage applications to its consumer lending personnel. These staff members called each borrower and explained to them that they also qualified for the home-equity credit line. The borrower was asked how he or she would like to access the credit line.

    Initial results showed that 40 percent accepted the credit line. The institution felt very strongly that the home-equity line was a consumer lending product and should not be treated like a mortgage loan. The institution was willing to go up to a 90 percent loan-to-value ratio.

3. A commercial bank in the northeast offered all mortgage applicants a $5,000 line of credit that was secured by the home. The dollar limit kept the loan-to-value ratio low. Forty percent of applicants accepted the credit line, and 90 percent of those with the credit line drew it down within three months.

This cross-selling strategy is designed to be conservative on the loan-to-value ratio and to supply funds to new homeowners, who generally have strong borrowing needs. By placing the second lien on the property early, it decreases the likelihood that the borrowers will seek a credit line elsewhere after they have accumulated a significant amount of equity.

Cross-Sales to Existing Mortgage Customers: Cross-selling to existing mortgage customers has been one of the most effective promotional strategies employed by other financial institutions. It is particularly effective when coupled with a temporary price promotion. Response rates to personalized direct-mail solicitation range from 2 percent to 14 percent.

This case study's financial institution will mail solicitations to all mortgage holders who have been in their home five years or more, or who put more than 20 percent down. Mailings will be staggered and prioritized according to the amount of estimated equity available.

EXHIBIT 8.18

Mortgage Customer Equity Mailing Priority Sheet

Mtg#	Appraisal Value	Orig. Loan	Current Balance	Orig. amt. - Balance = Est. equity	Open Date
5	0	$650,000	$341,691	$308,309	1973135
9	0	$200,000	$0	$200,000	1983027
6	0	$130,000	$ 37,226	$ 92,774	1978213
7	0	$ 22,500	$ 10,109	$ 12,391	1969074
12	0	$ 14,000	$ 6,634	$ 7,966	1972288
1	0	$ 45,000	$ 37,072	$ 7,928	1976026
16	0	$ 35,000	$ 27,312	$ 7,688	1974274
4	0	$ 25,000	$ 17,336	$ 7,664	1983006
2	0	$ 18,000	$ 10,000	$ 7,292	1971197
8	475000	$250,000	$242,727	$ 7,273	1985361
13	0	$ 25,000	$ 17,791	$ 7,209	1973001
3	0	$ 43,000	$ 36,488	$ 7,012	1976010
18	0	$ 35,000	$ 29,451	$ 5,549	1977241
10	0	$ 25,000	$ 20,726	$ 4,274	1977119
17	0	$ 25,000	$ 20,781	$ 4,219	1977161
15	0	$185,000	$182,214	$ 2,786	1986098
14	0	$ 25,000	$ 22,644	$ 2,356	1979151
11	140000	$ 35,617	$ 93,299	($ 57,682)	1985350

Estimated equity can be calculated in a simple manner using a marketing customer information file to subtract current mortgage balances from original loan amounts, or appraisal values. Exhibit 8.18 shows a priority sheet derived from such a file.

Product Summary

- Because approximately one-third of home-equity is tax deductible, the benefits of home-equity credit products should be promoted.

- According to FIMA/Raddon National Research, the demand for home-equity loans is greatest among the following market segments: high-income, middle-income, thirty-five to forty-four year olds, trendy credit buyers, and accumulator leaders.

- Preferences for line-of-credit versus fixed-payment loans are virtually equal. However, the reasons for using the line-of-credit product differ according to targeted market.

- Two products should be offered: a revolving line-of-credit and an amortizing loan. The two products should be positioned according to the targeted market.

Targeted Market	Product	Positioning
High income	Line	Retain tax deduction
Middle income	Loan	Auto purchase
		Home Improvement

Credit Card Access: While credit-card access to home-equity credit does not appear to be in great demand, there are institutions successfully offering it to their client base. Promoted as a convenience service, it positions the institution's product apart from others. There is very little difference to the institution regarding costs—credit-card costs are quite similar to check-processing costs.

Pricing: Based on the profit maximization model, Exhibit 8.16, the home-equity loan will be priced at prime, plus 2 percent, with no closing costs.

Promotion: The following promotional strategies will be used:

1. Direct mail to targeted noncustomer households. Lists can be purchased through various firms nationwide. Specific demographic criteria (age, income, etc.) can be requested as well as geographic criteria (zip code, city, etc.).

2. Cross-sales to new mortgage applicants. Mortgage originators should be prepared, informed, and trained to cross-sell home-equity lines to qualified new mortgage customers.

3. Cross-sales to existing mortgage customers. Lists will be taken off marketing customer information files for direct-mail promotions.

Appendix A

Opportunity Analysis Pricing Model

Pricing Analysis Methodology
Pricing Analysis Evaluation Process

Appendix B

Media Usage Research Tables

Television Viewing Habits
Radio Listening Habits
Newspaper Habits

Appendix C

Example of Consumer Research

Appendix D

Samples of Product Development Worksheets

Appendix A:

Opportunity Analysis Pricing Model

Most financial institutions do not have readily available the resources to perform a complex analysis of current product-pricing or prospective-pricing alternatives. The institutions must rely on their own data-processing or service bureau processor to develop the data base required for opportunity analysis pricing. In some instances, financial institutions may be required to sample their customers account base for the data required to complete the pricing analysis.

Pricing Analysis Methodology

The following pricing analysis methodology can be utilized by financial institutions of all sizes. The focus of the model is explicit rather than driven by relationship pricing. However, the pricing information developed still facilitates decision making by reducing the process to a factual rather than an opinion basis.

The development of price adjustment recommendations includes the following steps:

Step 1   Complete product deposit-balance range stratifications of account data developed through data-processing or account-base sampling. This data should be collected by product-type code.

Step 2   Identify assumption data requirements and sources.

Step 3   Analyze the current profitability trends for each account-type deposit stratification level. Utilize the most recent Federal Reserve functional cost analysis data and/or data on cost and revenue developed by the financial institution.

Step 4   Examine competitive pricing data for the local marketplace(s) served by the financial institution to develop pricing alternatives.

Step 5   Complete a financial analysis pro forma that quantifies the net opportunity for income improvement with service-charge fees and the net opportunity for earnings' improvement after discounting lost-opportunity income that is associated with each pricing alternative.

235

Pricing Analysis Evaluation Process

Development of Account Deposit Stratification Data

Per-Account Data: The core data, per account, to be extracted through the financial institution's data-processing system includes the following:

- Minimum ledger balance, within full statement cycle

- Average ledger balance, within full statement cycle

- Average collected balance, within full statement cycle

- Number of debits for complete statement cycle

- Number of credits for complete statement cycle

- Sum of NSFs/ODs (items) for complete statement cycle or aggregate total for year-to-date

It is important that this data be collected for complete statement-cycle periods rather than be a one-day snapshot of account totals and activity levels. Most financial institutions will match up the activity history for the prior month's statement with deposit-balance stratification data. Data collection requires the aggregating of one full month's series of statement cycle to ensure that complete data is available for analysis.

Data Collection Sort Patterns: Deposit-balance stratification data and activity data for account is sorted by product-type code or service-charge calculation code. The account-type deposit balances are stratified as either "Minimum Balance," "Average Balance," or both. The reports generated are typically further sorted by account statuses of "Service Charge Reviewed" and "Service Charge Waived" to eliminate distortions of the pricing adjustment forecast.

Deposit-Balance Stratification Specifications: Table 1 gives an example of the stratifications that should be drawn from the data. It is important to stratify account deposit balances to accommodate every possible service-charge price point. The stratification levels that follow provide an excellent base for sorting account data into any required pricing stratification level.

Account deposit-balance stratifications for regular savings should be more finely arrayed at the lower end of the deposit-balance spectrum.

Table 1

Account Deposit-Balance Stratification

Less than 0.00		
0.00	to	99.99
100.00	to	199.99
200.00	to	249.99
250.00	to	299.99
300.00	to	399.99
400.00	to	499.99
500.00	to	599.99
600.00	to	699.99
700.00	to	749.99
750.00	to	799.99
800.00	to	899.99
900.00	to	999.99
1,000.00	to	1,249.99
1,250.00	to	1,499.99
1,500.00	to	1,999.99
2,000.00	to	2,499.99
2,500.00	to	2,999.99
3,000.00	to	3,999.99
4,000.00	to	4,999.99
5,000.00	to	7,499.99
7,500.00	to	9,999.99
10,000.00	to	14,999.99
15,000.00	to	19,999.99
20,000.00	to	24,999.99
25,000.00	to	49,999.99
50,000.00	to	99,999.99
100,000.00 or greater		

Opportunity Analysis Pricing Model

TABLE 2

Account Profitability Analysis Assumptions

BUDGET PROJECTIONS:

Interest Income % (Tax Equiv)	_____%
or Total Earning Asset Yield % Rate	_____%
Corporate Internal Funds Transfer % Rate	_____%

Forecast Cost-of-Funds % Rates:

- Regular Savings _____%
- NOW Accounts _____%
- SuperNOW (Money Market Checking) _____%
- Money Market Deposit Account (Limited) _____%
- Special High Interest Money Market Accts _____%
- CDs < $100M _____%
- CDs ≥ $100M _____%

Forecast Federal Funds Rate:

- Purchased _____%
- Sold _____%

ACCOUNT EXPENSE DATA

[   ]   Utilize Federal Reserve Bank Functional Cost Analysis Data

[   ]   Other (please specify)

Per Debit Cost	_____
Per Credit Cost	_____
Per Month Maint.	_____
Regular Savings	_____
Annual Expense	_____

COMPENSATING BALANCE EARNING CREDIT RATE %   _____%

RESERVE REQUIREMENT % RATES: (please check)

Demand Deposit Account Balances	[ ] 12%	[ ] 3%	[ ] Other ___%
NOW/SuperNOW Account Balances	[ ] 12%	[ ] 3%	[ ] Other ___%
Non-Personal Savings/Money Market Deposit Accounts	[ ] 3%	[ ] Other ___%	

This provides the data necessary to factor out of earnings' improvement projections small-balance, dormant accounts that will ultimately be taken off the books through service charges, once the price adjustments have been implemented.

Pricing Analysis Assumptions

Table 2 identifies the financial assumptions required for completing the pricing analysis.

Current Profitability Analysis

Values must be assigned to the various factor that determine account profitability. Typically, there are four sets of factors that influence current account profitability:

1. Definition of service-charge fee parameters (see Table 3)

2. Other profit (loss) factors such as interest payment, account balance basis; internal transfer rate, or average earning asset rate, for funds on deposit; and NSF/OD fee-income recognition (see Table 3)

3. Account cost factors associated with the monthly maintenance and activity level (see Table 3)

4. Factor values used in the calculation formulas to determine per-account expense and income

All of the profit (loss) factors are translated into a per-account comparison for each stratification level (see Table 4). Expense and income sources are combined to produce a per-account and aggregate accounts profit (loss) for each stratification of deposit-balance level.

Review Compilation of Competitive Pricing Data

Regardless of a financial institution's intention to offer its product line on a profitable basis, few can ignore the competitive realities of the marketplace in which it must compete. Most pricing decisions that are intended to improve profitability must be tempered by competitive price positioning.

The key issue is to ensure possession of current, detailed, and accurate pricing information about the institution's key competitors for the product(s) under review. Competitive pricing surveys should, at a

Table 3

Factors Determining Account Profitability

Minimum Balance Range	Service Charge	% Interest Paid
Less than $100	$7.00	0.00%
$100 to $199	$7.00	0.00%
$200 to $249	$7.00	0.00%
$250 to $299	$7.00	0.00%
$300 to $499	$7.00	0.00%
$500 to $599	$0.00	0.00%
$600 to $699	$0.00	0.00%
$700 to $799	$0.00	0.00%
$800 to $899	$0.00	0.00%
$900 to $999	$0.00	0.00%
$1,000 to $4,999	$0.00	0.00%
$5,000 to $9,999	$0.00	0.00%
$10,000 to $19,999	$0.00	0.00%
$20,000 to $24,999	$0.00	0.00%
$25,000 and over	$0.00	0.00%

Other Factors

Interest pay basis %	=	100.00%
Interest trans rate %	=	6.03%
Investable balance %	=	88.00%
NSF/OD charge	=	$15.00
NSF collection %	=	85.00%

Account Costs

Account maintenance	=	$6.30
Cost/debit	=	$0.23
Cost/credit	=	$0.49

Per Item Charges

Minimum balance required	=	$500.00
Price/debit	=	$0.00
Price/credit	=	$0.00
Number of free items	=	0

TABLE 4

TYPE ACCOUNT: 01/PERSONAL DDA - REVIEWED

MINIMUM BALANCE RANGE	NUMBER OF ACCOUNT	AVERAGE BALANCE PER ACCT	DEBITS PER ACCOUNT	CREDITS PER ACCOUNT	INTEREST EXPENSE PER ACCT	COST PER ACCOUNT	BALANCE INCOME PER ACCT	SC INCOME PER ACCT	PROFIT/ (LOSS) PER ACCT	TOTAL/ PROFIT (LOSS)
LESS THAN $100	6075	368.78	19.91	2.76	0.00	12.23	1.63	7.00	-3.60	......
$100 TO $199	1472	622.66	24.97	3.08	0.00	13.55	2.75	7.00	-3.80	-5590.10
$200 TO $249	549	807.26	25.76	·	0.00	13.67	3.57	7.00	-3.10	·
·	431	961.18	·	·	·	13.69	4.25	7.00	-2.44	·
·	1267	1273.63	·	·	·	·	5.63	7.00	·	·
·	·	·	·	·	·	·	·	·	·	·
$25000 AND OVER	·	·	18.73	2.84	0.00	12.00	12.18	·	376.56	54977.49
Total or Average	16305	27.53.54	22.29	2.82	0.00	12.81	12.18	4.20	3.57	58243.18

241

Opportunity Analysis Pricing Model

TABLE 5

NOW Checking Account

INSTITUTION:

YOUR INSTITUTION:

ACCOUNT CRITERIA:

Balance Basis For: | Service Charges | Interest Payment
Minimum (Low) Ledger ☐ ☐
Average Ledger ☐ ☐
Minimum (Low) Collected ☐ ☐
Average Collected ☐ ☐
Other _____ ☐ ☐

SERVICE CHARGE CALCULATION:

THE BALANCE IS:		Monthly Maint Fee	# Free Dr	ITEM CHARGES		
AT LEAST	BUT LESS THAN			Per Dr	Per Cr	Per Dr & Cr

INTEREST PAYMENT RATES:

THE BALANCE IS:		Interest Rate %	Comp Method
AT LEAST	BUT LESS THAN		
	(max. rate)	%	
		%	
		%	
(lowest rate)		%	

Regular Savings Account

INSTITUTION:

COMPETITION:

ACCOUNT CRITERIA:

Balance Basis For: | Service Charges | Interest Payment
Minimum (Low) Ledger ☐ ☐
Average Ledger ☐ ☐
Minimum (Low) Collected ☐ ☐
Average Collected ☐ ☐
Other _____ ☐ ☐

Requirements to Avoid Service Charge:
Circle Statement Frequency: M Q SA A

Exemptions:
☐ Minors
☐ Seniors
☐ Others _____

SERVICE CHARGE CALCULATION:

THE BALANCE IS:		Monthly Maint Fee	# Free Withdrawals For Statement	Excess Withdrawal Charge
AT LEAST	BUT LESS THAN			

INTEREST PAYMENT RATES:

THE BALANCE IS:		Interest Rate %	Comp Method
AT LEAST	BUT LESS THAN		
	(max. rate)	%	
		%	
		%	
(lowest rate)		%	

Personal Checking Account

INSTITUTION:

YOUR INSTITUTION:

ACCOUNT CRITERIA:

Balance Basis For: | Service Charges | Interest Payment
Minimum (Low) Ledger ☐ ☐
Average Ledger ☐ ☐
Minimum (Low) Collected ☐ ☐
Average Collected ☐ ☐
Other _____ ☐ ☐

Requirements to Avoid Service Charge:

SERVICE CHARGE CALCULATION:

THE BALANCE IS:		Monthly Maint Fee	# Free Dr	ITEM CHARGES		
AT LEAST	BUT LESS THAN			Per Dr	Per Cr	Per Dr & Cr

minimum, be conducted semiannually to provide the needed competitive perspective for management's decisions about product pricing. Table 5 illustrates a format for competitive survey data compilation for several types of financial products.

Service-Charge-Fee Scenario Assumptions

Scenario values are assigned to each of the four principal factor-clusters identified in the current profitability analysis. A new set of key assumptions is introduced into the service-charge-fee scenario analysis. An account run-off projection table is built for each service-charge-fee/ interest rate adjustment scenario following the review of the competitive pricing survey data. The factor clusters are

1. The scenario service-charge-fee criteria (see Table 6)

2. The percentage of accounts, by deposit-balance stratification range, expected to remain if the scenario pricing criteria were implemented (see Table 6).

3. Other profit (loss) factors such as interest-payment, account-balance basis; internal transfer rate, or average earning asset rate, for funds on deposit; and NSF/OD fee-income recognition (see Table 6)

4. Account cost factors associated with monthly maintenance and account activity level (see Table 6)

5. Factor values used in the calculation formulas to determine per-account expense and income

Service-Charge-Fee Scenario Analysis

All of the profit (loss) factors are similarly translated into a per-account comparison for each stratification level to reflect the scenario's changes (see Table 7). Expense and income sources are revised to produce a scenario per-account and aggregate accounts profit (loss) for each stratification deposit-balance level.

The net change in service-charge fee between the current service charge and scenario service charge should be a key factor in the scenario evaluation process. The net change after further discounting the fee-revenue change by lost-opportunity income adds a conservative dimension to the evaluation process. Lost-opportunity income is derived from

Opportunity Analysis Pricing Model

TABLE 6

Minimum Balance Range	Service Charge	% Interest Paid	% Retain
Less than $100	$4.95	0.00%	95.00%
$100 to $199	$4.95	0.00%	95.00%
$200 to $249	$4.95	0.00%	95.00%
$250 to $299	$4.95	0.00%	95.00%
$300 to $499	$4.95	0.00%	90.00%
$500 to $599	$0.00	0.00%	100.00%
$600 to $699	$0.00	0.00%	100.00%
$700 to $799	$0.00	0.00%	100.00%
$800 to $899	$0.00	0.00%	100.00%
$900 to $999	$0.00	0.00%	100.00%
$1,000 to $4,999	$0.00	0.00%	100.00%
$5,000 to $9,999	$0.00	0.00%	100.00%
$10,000 to $19,999	$0.00	0.00%	100.00%
$20,000 to $24,999	$0.00	0.00%	100.00%
$25,000 and over	$0.00	0.00%	100.00%

Other Factors

Interest Pay Basis %	=	88.00%
Interest Trans Rate %	=	6.03%
Investable Balance %	=	88.00%
NSF/OD Charge	=	$15.00
NSF Collection %	=	85.00%

Account Costs

Account Maintenance	=	$6.30
Cost/Debit	=	$0.23
Cost/Credit	=	$0.49

Per Item Charges

Minimum Balance Requir.	=	$500
Price/Debit	=	$0.20
Price/Credit	=	$0.20
# Free Items	=	0

244

TABLE 7

MINIMUM BALANCE RANGE	NUMBER OF ACCOUNT	AVERAGE BALANCE PER ACCT	DEBITS PER ACCOUNT	CREDITS PER ACCOUNT	INTEREST EXPENSE PER ACCT	COST PER ACCOUNT	BALANCE INCOME PER ACCT	SC INCOME PER ACCT	PROFIT/ (LOSS) PER ACCT	TOTAL/ PROFIT (LOSS)
LESS THAN $100	5771.3	368.78	19.91	2.76	0.00	12.23	1.63	9.48	-1.12	-6451.80
$100 TO $199	1398.4	622.66	24.97	.	0.00	13.55	2.75	10.56	-0.24	-332.40
$200 TO $249	521.6	807.26	25.74	.	0.00	13.67	3.57	10.69	0.59	308.84
. . . . .	409.5	961.18	.	.	.	13.69	4.25	10.69	1.25	.
	1140.3						5.63	10.61	2.69	
							5.33	0.00		
								0.00		
								0.00		
$25000 AND OVER	.	.	.	.	.	11.43	.	0.00	105.33	18206.81
						12.00	388.55	0.00	376.56	5477.14
										54977.49
Total or Average	.	.	.	.	.	12.81	12.50	5.81	5.51	186739.52

NET CHANGE

	SERVICE CHARGE	RUNOFF
	12214	9279
	4463	4045
	1733	1586
	1361	1231
	.	2252
	.	0
	22996	18393
	0	0
	0	0

245

the value of deposit-balance runoff and prospective, lost-NSF/OD fee-income associated with accounts consolidated or closed by customers because of the price adjustment.

The analysis of comparative service-charge adjustment scenarios should exclude any reflection of theoretical expense reductions associated with the reduction in account base. Most financial institutions' experiences suggest that these types of expense reductions are difficult to capture even though a logical case can be made for their probable existence. The comparative merits of different service-charge routine scenarios should be purely based upon their impact on revenue rather than on anticipated reductions of expenses that are associated with implementation.

Appendix B:

Media Usage Research Tables

The tables in this appendix are the result of national research conducted by the FIMA/Raddon Strategic Research and Planning Program.

Media Usage Research Tables

Television Watching Habits

- Age -

Daily Time Spent Watching TV	Total	18-34	35-44	45-54	55-64	65 +
Less than 1 hour	7%	9%	9%	8%	5%	4%
1 hour to 3 hours	41%	45%	(53%)	37%	38%	33%
3 hours or more	50%	46%	38%	53%	57%	58%
Average (hours)	3.63	3.60	[3.38]	3.71	3.87	3.81
Peak Watching Time - % Watching						
8 p.m. - 10 p.m.	68%	69%	(76%)	69%	70%	62%
6 p.m. - 8 p.m.	53%	48%	42%	58%	58%	(64%)
10 p.m. - Midnight	34%	34%	32%	36%	38%	35%
6 a.m. - 8 a.m.	14%	12%	13%	14%	15%	13%
Type of Stations Primarily Watched						
Major Networks	78%	72%	77%	80%	85%	82%
Public Broadcasting	25%	19%	17%	26%	(33%)	31%
Cable Programming	24%	21%	29%	28%	29%	18%
Independent Local	14%	9%	10%	16%	17%	20%
Type of Programming Most Frequently Watched						
Local News	54%	38%	47%	(65%)	(65%)	59%
National Network News	35%	21%	27%	37%	(45%)	(47%)
Situation Comedies	31%	(50%)	34%	30%	23%	19%
Game Shows	23%	16%	17%	18%	29%	(36%)
Sporting Events	20%	17%	19%	(28%)	20%	21%

Television Viewing Habits—Age

Comments:

The average consumer watches 3.63 hours of television a day. Older consumers watch more television a day than younger consumers, which makes television advertising attractive for those targeting a customer over fifty-five.

Prime time is the most-watched time period by each segment, except those sixty-five and over. The over sixty-five market views television between 6 p.m. and 8 p.m. and between 8 p.m. and 10 p.m. an equal amount.

While almost 80 percent said that they primarily watch the major networks (ABC, NBC, and CBS), almost one-quarter of the respondents said that they watch cable programming—where buying time is less expensive. The thirty-five to sixty-four age group is more likely to watch cable.

Advertising for asset products should focus on situation comedies. One-half of the eighteen to thirty-four year-olds reported that situation comedies are the most-often-watched programing type. Deposit-product advertising would be most effective during local or national news programming. A key IRA market, those in the forty-five to fifty-four age group, would be most-effectively reached by advertising during televised sporting events.

Media Usage Research Tables

Television Watching Habits

- Balance, Income -

		Balance			Income		
Daily Time Spent Watching TV	Total	Less than $10K	$10K to $25K	$25K or More	Less than $25K	$25K to $50K	$50K or More
Less than 1 hour	7%	8%	5%	7%	5%	8%	12%
1 hour to 3 hours	41%	40%	47%	38%	32%	50%	49%
3 hours or more	50%	51%	47%	53%	60%	42%	39%
Average	3.63	3.78	3.44	3.70	(4.11)	3.27	3.25
Peak Watching Time % Watching							
8 p.m. - 10 p.m.	68%	69%	69%	72%	67%	73%	71%
6 p.m. - 8 p.m.	53%	49%	54%	(62%)	55%	51%	52%
10 p.m. - Midnight	34%	35%	33%	40%	34%	33%	(44%)
6 a.m. - 8 a.m.	14%	13%	14%	16%	13%	13%	16%
Type of Stations Primarily Watched							
Major Networks	78%	76%	80%	(85%)	79%	80%	77%
Public Broadcasting	25%	20%	28%	(31%)	26%	23%	24%
Cable Programming	24%	27%	21%	24%	23%	25%	29%
Independent Local	14%	14%	17%	13%	18%	12%	8%
Type of Programming Most Frequently Watched							
Local News	54%	50%	55%	61%	55%	55%	46%
National Network News	35%	29%	34%	47%	35%	33%	39%
Situation Comedies	31%	37%	27%	27%	33%	33%	24%
Game Shows	23%	24%	20%	24%	30%	16%	18%
Sporting Events	20%	17%	20%	28%	15%	23%	(31%)

Television Viewing Habits—Balance, Income

Comments:

In order to most-efficiently reach the high-balance market, institutions should concentrate on the 6-p.m. to 8-p.m. time spot. This is not as expensive as the prime time slot but shows significantly higher viewing by this balance group.

The high-income group watches less television than any other segment. Therefore, it is necessary to pinpoint their specific viewing style to reach members of this group. Advertising during the 10-p.m. to midnight time spot or during sporting events would be most effective.

Television Watching Habits
- Cluster -

	Total	Service Assurance Seekers	Trendy Credit Buyers	Accumulator Leader	Ambitious Security Driven	People Oriented Traditionalist	Institution Dependents	Convenience Driven	Price Alert
Daily Time Spent Watching TV									
Less than 1 hour	7%	2%	5%	(14%)	5%	5%	3%	9%	10%
1 hour to 3 hours	41%	40%	42%	46%	43%	31%	40%	46%	42%
3 hours or more	50%	55%	51%	39%	53%	55%	55%	42%	47%
Average	3.63	3.72	3.79	3.25	3.76	3.87	3.70	3.37	3.52
Peak Watching Time % Watching									
8 p.m. - 10 p.m.	68%	72%	65%	73%	(79%)	62%	68%	64%	67%
6 p.m. - 8 p.m.	53%	54%	50%	53%	57%	54%	51%	51%	53%
10 p.m. - Midnight	34%	30%	35%	32%	31%	37%	33%	34%	(41%)
6 a.m. - 8 a.m.	14%	11%	12%	18%	8%	13%	(19%)	11%	14%
Types of Stations Primarily Watched									
Major Networks	78%	82%	76%	(82%)	80%	82%	77%	72%	77%
Public Broadcasting	25%	20%	18%	30%	30%	22%	22%	24%	30%
Cable Programming	24%	28%	29%	24%	22%	19%	25%	24%	25%
Independent Local	14%	12%	16%	9%	18%	16%	15%	13%	13%
Type of Programming Most Frequently Watched									
Local News	54%	53%	48%	55%	57%	50%	(61%)	51%	54%
National Network News	35%	33%	29%	35%	35%	35%	39%	26%	(43%)
Situation Comedies	31%	30%	(41%)	29%	40%	23%	29%	35%	24%
Game Shows	23%	15%	26%	21%	28%	30%	20%	25%	18%
Sporting Events	20%	17%	18%	(29%)	23%	14%	25%	13%	22%

Television Viewing Habits—Cluster

Comments:

Price Alerts, Trendy Credit Buyers, and Accumulator Leaders are the most attractive borrowing segments. Trendy Credit Buyers watch the most television per day (3.79 hours on average). Price Alerts watch slightly less television a day on average but are more likely to watch after 10 p.m. Accumulator Leaders re more likely to watch the major networks. In order to most-efficiently market loan products to these segments through television, concentration should be placed on situation comedy programming for Trendy Credit Buyers, on national news for Price Alerts, and on sporting events for Accumulator Leaders.

To most-effectively market deposit products, concentration should be placed on the Price Alerts, Institution Dependents, and Accumulator Leaders. The Institution Dependents can be reached most efficiently through the local news and are more likely to watch television between 6 a.m. and 8 a.m. than are the other cluster groups.

Television Viewing—
Segment Reach Indices

Index 100 = Average

Programming	Age % of			Income % of		
	Group	Listeners	Index	Group	Listeners	Index
Local news	55–64	23%	(122)	<$25K	50%	103
	45–54	17%	121	$25K–$50K	34%	103
National network news	65+	29%	136	<$25K	49%	100
	55–64	25%	129			
Situation comedies	18–34	27%	130	<$25K	60%	124
	35–44	22%	105			
Game shows	65+	33%	(154)	<$25K	64%	132
	55–64	24%	124			
Sporting events	45–54	20%	138	$50K+	22%	(154)
				$25K–$50K	38%	115

Comments:

The index is computed to show above-average media use for a type of programming by a particular group. For example, an institution would be 22 percent more likely to reach a 55 to 64 year-old when advertising on local news. This group makes up 23 percent of the local news viewers.

Television Viewing—
Segment Reach Indices

Index 100 = Average

Programming	Balance % of			Clusters % of		
	Segment	Watchers	Index	Segment	Watchers	Index
Local news	$25K+	29%	115	Tradit.	15%	94%
				Inst. Dep.	14%	(113)
				Price Alert	14%	100
National network news	$25K+	34%	136	Price Aler	17%	123
				Tradit.	16%	101
				Inst. Dep.	14%	112
Situation comedies	<$10K	57%	121	Trndy Crd.	19%	(131)
				Amb. Sec.	14%	128
				Accu. Ldr.	13%	19
Game show	<$25K	49%	106	Tradit.	20%	(140)
				Trndy Crd.	16%	98
				Amb. Sec.	13%	85
Sporting events	$25K+	35%	(139)	Accu. Ldr.	19%	(141)
				Inst. Dep.	16%	122
				Price Alert	16%	110

Comments:

Sporting events attract an affluent crowd. They have high-balance and high-incomes and present both good borrowing and deposit-product potential in terms of cluster identification.

Radio Listening Habits

- Age -

Daily Time Spent Listening	Total	18-34	35-44	45-54	55-64	65 +
Less than 1 hour	30%	26%	30%	35%	31%	34%
1 to 2 hours	24%	23%	26%	18%	27%	24%
2 to 3 hours	11%	14%	14%	11%	6%	11%
3 hours or more	28%	(35%)	29%	32%	30%	16%
No Response	7%	2%	1%	4%	6%	15%
Peak Listening Time - % Listening						
6 a.m. - 8 a.m.	43%	45%	(57%)	48%	40%	26%
8 a.m. - 9 a.m.	29%	34%	31%	27%	28%	27%
4 p.m. - 6 p.m.	22%	31%	25%	29%	21%	8%
10 a.m. - Noon	20%	26%	20%	20%	18%	17%
Frequency Primarily Listened To						
AM	17%	7%	11%	20%	23%	(27%)
FM	48%	(75%)	52%	51%	40%	23%
Both	30%	16%	37%	27%	34%	(39%)
Program Format						
Easy Listening	33%	9%	18%	46%	51%	50%
Country & Western	27%	16%	31%	33%	34%	25%
Soft Rock	20%	46%	33%	10%	8%	2%
Talk/Variety	14%	6%	10%	12%	24%	20%

Radio Listening Habits—Age

Comments:

The average time spent listening to the radio is inversely related to age. Peak listening times are the "drive" times and do not vary significantly, except for the 6 a.m. to 8 a.m. slot when the thirty-five-to-forty-four-age group is 32 percent more likely to listen. FM frequency is more often listened to than AM, except in the sixty-five-and-over group.

The top four program formats are easy listening (33%), country and western (27%), soft rock (20%) and talk variety (14%). Soft rock is more appealing to the younger age groups; easy listening and talk/variety, to the older groups.

Radio Listening Habits

		Balance			Income		
Daily Time Spent Listening	Total	Less than $10K	$10K to $25K	$25K or More	Less than $25K	$25K to $50K	$50K or More
Less than 1 hour	30%	29%	33%	34%	28%	33%	34%
1 to 2 hours	24%	23%	26%	25%	22%	26%	27%
2 to 3 hours	11%	13%	10%	7%	10%	13%	10%
3 hours or more	28%	30%	28%	26%	31%	25%	28%
No Response	7%	5%	3%	7%	9%	3%	1%
Peak Listening Time % Listening							
6 a.m. - 8 a.m.	43%	42%	48%	45%	35%	48%	(60%)
8 a.m. - 9 a.m.	29%	30%	31%	28%	28%	32%	31%
4 p.m. - 6 p.m.	22%	22%	25%	22%	17%	27%	(33%)
10 a.m. - Noon	20%	21%	19%	22%	21%	21%	18%
Frequency Primarily Listened to							
AM	17%	14%	17%	(25%)	19%	17%	14%
FM	48%	(55%)	44%	41%	45%	51%	53%
Both	30%	27%	37%	30%	30%	31%	31%
Program Format							
Easy Listening	33%	26%	32%	(47%)	34%	33%	29%
Country & Western	27%	30%	25%	21%	(32%)	25%	18%
Soft Rock	20%	(26%)	19%	13%	17%	25%	(25%)
Talk/Variety	14%	10%	17%	(22%)	14%	16%	14%

258

Radio Listening Habits—Balance, Income

Comments:

In order to reach the high-balance segment, marketers should concentrate on AM stations, easy listening, and talk program formats. The peak listening times do not vary significantly for the high-balance segment and the overall market.

The high-income group is more likely to listen to the radio between 6 A.M. and 8 A.M. and between 4 P.M. and 6 P.M. Soft Rock is the program format that is most likely to reach this group.

Media Usage Research Tables

Radio Listening Habits
- Cluster Groups -

	Total	Service Assurance Seekers	Trendy Credit Buyers	Accumulator Leader	Ambitious Security Driven	People Oriented Traditionalist	Institution Dependents	Convenience Driven	Price Alert
Daily Time Spent Watching TV									
Less than 1 hour	30%	29%	25%	(36%)	30%	26%	29%	34%	33%
1 to 2 hours	24%	28%	23%	27%	31%	20%	22%	26%	22%
2 to 3 hours	11%	13%	15%	11%	12%	10%	8%	11%	8%
3 hours or more	28%	23%	32%	21%	23%	30%	(35%)	21%	(35%)
No Response	7%	7%	5%	4%	5%	15%	6%	9%	2%
Peak Listening Time % Listening									
6 a.m. - 8 a.m.	43%	49%	48%	38%	42%	33%	39%	48%	48%
8 a.m. - 9 a.m.	29%	30%	27%	26%	29%	(36%)	29%	23%	33%
4 p.m. - 6 p.m.	22%	22%	29%	31%	16%	[14%]	22%	19%	24%
10 a.m. - Noon	20%	16%	23%	25%	19%	20%	19%	21%	18%
Frequency Primarily Listened to									
AM	17%	20%	14%	15%	19%	(23%)	16%	16%	15%
FM	48%	46%	(57%)	(56%)	46%	33%	47%	55%	44%
Both	30%	32%	25%	27%	32%	31%	31%	23%	39%
Program Format									
Easy Listening	33%	26%	[21%]	41%	42%	31%	36%	32%	35%
Country Western	27%	25%	27%	23%	24%	(36%)	24%	37%	[19%]
Soft Rock	20%	25%	(31%)	23%	15%	5%	19%	23%	(25%)
Talk/Variety	14%	11%	11%	14%	(20%)	16%	15%	9%	15%

Radio Listening Habits—Cluster Group

Comments:

Institution Dependents and Price Alerts are more likely to listen to the radio more than three hours a day. Both of these cluster groups are excellent users of deposit products.

Price Alerts tend to listen to soft rock and easy listening, and are significantly less likely to listen to country western.

Credit products would be most-efficiently advertised on soft rock stations where both Price Alerts and Trendy Credit Buyers report significantly higher listening.

Radio Listening—
Segment Reach Indices

Index 100 = Average

Programming	Age % of			Income % of		
	Group	Listeners	Index	Group	Listeners	Index
Easy listening	65+	33%	153			
	55-64	29%	153			
Country western	45-64	42%	125	<$25K	56%	117
Soft rock	18-34	47%	(224)	$25K-$50K	40%	121
Talk/Variety	55-64	32%	166	$25K-$50K	37%	111
	65+	30%	140			

Comments:

There was no income group with above-average listening in the easy listening category.

Advertising consumer credit should be more successful on stations with soft rock program formats.

Radio Listening—
Segment Reach Indices

Index 100 = Average

Programming	Balance % of			Cluster % of		
	Group	Listeners	Index	Group	Listeners	Index
Easy listening	$25K	36%	142	Accm. ldr.	17%	125
				Amb. sec.	13%	123
				Price alert	15%	105
Country western	<$10K	52%	116	Tradit.	21%	132
Soft rock	<$10K	60%	127	Trndy. cr.	22%	(153)
				Price alert	17%	123
				Serv. assr.	11%	123
				Accm. ldr.	15%	112
Talk/Variety	$25+	38%	138	Amb. sec.	15%	(144)
				Tradit.	18%	116
				Price alert	15%	109
				Inst. dep.	14%	109

Comments:

Easy listening is a good format for deposit product sales by virtue of its cluster segment listenership. The talk/variety format also has strong appeal for deposit relationships.

263

Newspaper Habits

Time Spent During the Day Reading the Newspaper

	Average Time (minutes)	Less than 15 minutes	15 minutes or more
Total	23	31%	65%
Balance			
Less than $10K	19	43%	55%
$10K–$25K	26	24%	74%
$25K or more	(28)	19%	(79%)
Income			
Less than $25K	22	33%	63%
$25K–$50K	23	33%	67%
$50K or more	26	27%	(72%)
Age			
18–34	16	53%	[46%]
35–44	20	41%	59%
45–54	24	27%	71%
55–64	27	19%	79%
65+	(29)	15%	(80%)

Comments:

While the average time spent reading the newspaper is twenty-three minutes, the most-attractive deposit groups (high-balance and older readers) spend more time. Credit product users spend less time than average on the newspaper.

Appendix C:

Example Of Customer Research

Dear Valued Customer:

We are constantly striving to improve our service and product offerings so that they may meet all of your financial needs.

We would like to learn more about you and your opinions. We have selected you at random to be a customer survey participant. The survey is strictly confidential and anonymous. Would you please take a few minutes to complete it and return it in the enclosed stamped envelope?

Your opinions will be representative of many others, so we appreciate your assistance in this project.

Thank you!

Sincerely,

President

Please have the person(s) in your family who is responsible for making household financial decisions complete the questionnaire.

1. Please circle the number next to the office you use most frequently.

Location 1	01	Food Store Offices	
Location 2	02	Store 1	11
Location 3	03	Store 2	12
Location 4	04	Store 3	13
Location 5	05	Store 4	14
Location 6	06	Store 5	15
Location 7	07	Store 6	16
Location 8	08	Store 7	17
Location 9	09		

1a. In the space provided, please indicate the number of the office you use second most frequently. If none, leave blank.

_____(INSERT NUMBER)

267

Example Of Customer Research

2. In the spaces provided, please indicate any other financial institutions that you are using. Also, indicate which institution is your primary, or most important, provider of financial services by checking the appropriate box.

Institutions Used Check	Primary Institution
Our institution	[ ]
_____	[ ]
_____	[ ]
_____	[ ]
_____	[ ]

3. Please think of what is important to you in selecting your primary financial institution to handle your most important personal financial business. For the following characteristics, would you please indicate if each is Extremely Important, Very Important, Somewhat Important, or Not at All Important? (PLEASE CIRCLE IMPORTANCE CHOICE FOR EACH)

	Extremely Important	Very Important	Somewhat Important	Not Important
Banking hours	4	3	2	1
Interest rates paid on deposits	4	3	2	1
Friendliness of staff	4	3	2	1
Format of account statements	4	3	2	1
Accuracy of account statements	4	3	2	1
Responsiveness to your needs	4	3	2	1
Convenience of locations	4	3	2	1
Speed of service	4	3	2	1
Availability of loans	4	3	2	1
Deposit incentives	4	3	2	1
Savers' Club benefits	4	3	2	1
Higher rates for larger balances	4	3	2	1
Frequency of compounding	4	3	2	1
Other _____	4	3	2	1
Other_____	4	3	2	1

4. Now, for each characteristic that is listed below, please rate us on how well we deliver on these characteristics. (CIRCLE RATING)

	Rating of Our Institution			
	Excellent	Good	Fair	Poor
Banking hours	4	3	2	1
Interest rates paid on deposits	4	3	2	1
Friendliness of staff	4	3	2	1
Format of account statements	4	3	2	1
Accuracy of account statements	4	3	2	1
Responsiveness to your needs	4	3	2	1
Convenience of locations	4	3	2	1
Speed of service	4	3	2	1
Availability of loans	4	3	2	1
Deposit incentives	4	3	2	1
Savers' Club benefits	4	3	2	1
Higher rates for larger balances	4	3	2	1
Frequency of compounding	4	3	2	1
Other _____	4	3	2	1
Other_____	4	3	2	1

5a. Do you use automatic teller machines?

(CIRCLE THE APPROPRIATE RESPONSE)

Yes   1

No   2

5b. Would you begin using automatic teller machines, or use them more frequently, if more locations were available?

(CIRCLE THE APPROPRIATE RESPONSE)

Yes   1

No   2

269

Example Of Customer Research

5c. Please indicate in the space below any location that you would like to have automatic teller machines available.

_____

_____

_____

6a. Please indicate the service that you are currently using by circling the number that corresponds to the service. If you use the service at our institution, circle the number in the left-hand column. If you use the service elsewhere, circle the number in the right-hand column. If you use the service at our institution and elsewhere, circle the numbers in both the left- and right-hand columns.

	Use at Our Institution	Use Service Elsewhere
Noninterest earning checking	1	1
5-1/4% NOW checking account	2	2
Market-rate SuperNOW checking account	3	3
Passbook savings account	4	4
Statement savings account	5	5
Automatic teller machine card	6	6
Money market deposit account	7	7
Certificate of deposit	8	8
Individual retirement account	9	9
Mortgage loan	0	0
Auto loan	-1	-1
Personal line of credit	-2	-2
Other_____	-3	-3
Other_____	-4	-4
Other_____	-5	-5
Other_____	-6	-6
None	-7	-7

270

6b. Please indicate the approximate total dollar amount of funds your household has at our institution and at other financial institutions. Add together funds from different account types and circle the number for the appropriate dollar group.

	Deposits at Our Institution	Deposits Held Elsewhere
Less than $1,000	1	1
$1,000 to $2,499	2	2
$2,500 to $4,999	3	3
$5,000 to $9,999	4	4
$10,000 to $14,999	5	5
$15,000 to $24,999	6	6
$25,000 or more	7	7

7. Regular savings accounts pay interest and allow deposits and withdrawals at any time. The account provides a passbook or a statement, and it pays a fixed rate of 5-1/4% or 5-1/2%.

Money market accounts are like savings accounts but pay a higher rate of interest. This rate may change each week depending on market conditions. These accounts generally require a minimum deposit of $1,000 or $2,500.

Which would you prefer? (CIRCLE NUMBER NEXT TO CHOICE)

A regular savings account that paid a higher rate of interest, say 6% or 6-1/2%   1

OR

A money market account with a minimum balance of $500   2

7a. With this account, would you prefer a passbook or a monthly statement? (CIRCLE NUMBER NEXT TO CHOICE)

Passbook   1
Statement   2

7b. With this account, would you prefer a guaranteed rate or a floating rate? (CIRCLE NUMBER NEXT TO CHOICE)

Guaranteed rate   1
Floating rate   2

Example Of Customer Research

7c. If another financial institution offered your preferred account and our institution did not, how likely would you be to open the account at another institution? Would you be. . . (CIRCLE NUMBER NEXT TO CHOICE)

Extremely likely	1
Very likely	2
Somewhat likely	3
Not at all likely	4

8. If our institution offered a "premium investor" money market account that paid a higher rate of interest for deposits of $25,000 or more, how likely would you be to open the account? Would you be. . . (CIRCLE NUMBER NEXT TO CHOICE)

Extremely likely	1
Very likely	2
Somewhat likely	3
Not at all likely	4

9. Financial institutions are considering offering a wide variety of new services. Circle the number of each service listed below that you would be interested in obtaining through us.

Interest in Obtaining

Stock mutual funds	1	Financial planning	9
Bond mutual funds	2	Insurance	0
Tax-free bond mutual funds	3	Estate planning	-1
Tax-deferred annuities	4	Tax planning	-2
Discount stockbrokerage	5	Tax preparation	-3
Full-service stockbrokerage	6	None	-4 (Skip to 10)
Retirement counseling	7		
A self-directed IRA through which you can trade stocks or bonds	8		

9a. What would be the source of the majority of your funds if you were to obtain these investments and services at our institution? (CIRCLE NUMBER NEXT TO CHOICE)

Funds on deposits at _____	1
Funds on deposit elsewhere	2
Current earnings	3

Finally, please answer the following questions about you and your household so that we may compare your answers with those of others we survey. Please circle the number next to the appropriate response for each question.

10. In which of the following categories does your age fall?

18 to 24	1	45 to 54	4
25 to 34	2	55 to 64	5
35 to 44	3	65 and over	6

11. What is your marital status?

Married	1	Separated	4
Single	2	Divorced	5
Widowed	3		

12. Which of the following would you say best describes your 1988 total annual family income from all sources?

Less than $8,000	1
$8,000 but less that $15,000	2
$15,000 but less than $20,000	3
$20,000 but less than $25,000	4
$25,000 but less than $35,000	5
$35,000 but less than $50,000	6
$50,000 but less than $75,000	7
$75,000 or more	8

13. Which of the following would you say best describes your total liquid financial assets; that is, the total amount in checking, savings, certificates of deposit, and money market funds or money market accounts?

Less than $1,000	1
$1,000 but less than $5,000	2
$5,000 but less than $10,000	3
$10,000 but less than $15,000	4
$15,000 but less than $20,000	5
$20,000 but less than $25,000	6
$25,000 or more	7

14. What is the occupation of the male head of your household?

_____

15. What is the occupation of the female head of your household?

_____

16. Do you have children below the age of 18 living at home?

Yes	1
No	2

Thanks again for your participation!

Appendix D:

Samples of Product Development Worksheets

The five sample worksheets in this appendix were presented earlier in this book as exhibits. They are included here for the convenience of appropriate personnel at financial institutions.

EXHIBIT 2.5

"The Product Marketing Plan Format"

PLAN NAME: TIME PERIOD:

PREPARER:

DATE:

INTRODUCTION:

PRODUCT
DESCRIPTION:

MARKETING
ENVIRONMENT:

MARKET
POTENTIAL:

STRATEGIES:

IMPLEMEN-
TATION:

OPTIONAL
ADDENDUM:

Samples of Product Development Worksheets

EXHIBIT 2.6

Action Plan Overview

Date: _____ **, 199___**

ACTION PLAN NAME: _____ I D # _____

SUBJECT REFERENCE: _____

_____

_____ I D # _____

STRATEGICAL APPROACH: _____

_____

_____

RESOURCE REQUIREMENTS: _____

_____

KEY PROGRESS CHECKPOINTS:

CHECKPOINT DESCRIPTION	ASSIGNED	PLAN SCHEDULE DATES			
		Start-Up	Progress Check	Projected Completion	Actual Completion

EXHIBIT 2.6a

Detailed Action Plan Schedule Summary

Week of:_____; Date: _____, 199__

PROJECT/TASK DESCRIPTION								

Samples of Product Development Worksheets

EXHIBIT 4.6

Product Line Gap Identification

Market Segment Type	Transaction Prod./Serv.	Savings/Investment Prod./Serv.	Credit Prod./Serv.	Retirement/Security Prod./Serv.

EXHIBIT 4.7
PRODUCT/SERVICES OPPORTUNITY EVALUATION

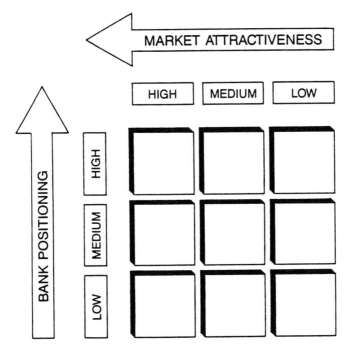

KEY: (H = High; M = Medium; L = Low)

Factor	Market Attractiveness	Bank Position	Factor	Market Attractiveness	Bank Position
1. Market Size			13. Skills Fit		
2. Market Growth			14. Product Synergism		
3. Segmentation Ease			15. Cyclical Synergism		
4. Penetration Cost			16. Profit Margins		
5. Market Share			17. Image Fit		
6. Defensive Motivation			18. Differentia-tion		
7. Entry Requirements			19. Capital Resources		
8. Competitive Climate			20. People Resources		
9. Regulatory/ Social Climate			21. Price Sensitivity		
10. Distribution System			22. On-Stream Time		
11. Systems/ Tech Barriers			23. Critical Volume		
12. Capacity			24. Entry